Poetic Tales from the Isle of Lewis

by

Colin Demét

Published by Wordcatcher Publications in 2005

Printed in the Isle of Lewis.

A catalogue record for this book
is available from the British Library

ISBN -10
0-9551318-0-4

ISBN -13
978-0-9551318-0-6

Cover Illustration of the King and Queen
from the Lewis Chessmen.
Design of cover by Colin and Annette Demét

Printed and bound on the Isle of Lewis by
Wordcatcher Publications
Loch á Tuath Cottage
Flesherin, Point,
Isle of Lewis, HS2 OHE

www.wordcatcherpublications.com

Contents

Contents (cont'd)
Part Two

Note from the Author

I would like to thank my wife, Annette for her patience, perseverance and the dedication she has given towards the publication of this book. Without her invaluable help this book would not exist today.

Colin Demet

ACKNOWLEDGEMENTS

Grateful thanks go to the many people of Lewis who whispered tales over tea and biscuits. One lady in particular we could not forget is Isabel (Bibby) Graham for her help with the Gaelic translations within the book.

We also would like to acknowledge and thank the people from the reference and historical department of the Stornoway Library for their patience, help and assistance.

Part One

Tales from the Gas House

Tigh - a - Ghas

I awoke to find I was sleeping.
It was dark yet the room was light.
I knew where I was, yet I was somewhere else.
The Wordcatcher sleeps tonight.

TALES FROM THE GAS HOUSE

The old cracked bell screamed like a banshee from Stornoway shipyard. One long, solitary haunting peel. Rev. R.M. Stephen whispered, 'I knew the bell would be found. I knew the bell would toll again in Portrona'.

TIGH - A - GHAS

The towering gas house chimney belched black smoke, like an old man's pipe, through the early morning mist. Stornoway was quiet, peaceful and still; as a child waking to greet a new day. The scent from smoking kippers floated through the streets of Stornoway to slowly creep, ghost-like over the surrounding land and sea.

John MacPhail was standing, as he often did, with one foot in the gas-house gate. It was as if he was trapped between the gas-house and the outside world - as if trying to escape, yet had nowhere to go. His face was black with soot and the dust of coal. John puffed hard on his pipe and stared intensely down the cobbled road which led to the gas-house gate.

Arched high above the two metal gas-house gates, resembling a satanic rainbow - foreboding and omnipotent - two words were written in large rusty iron letters, 'NO ADMITTANCE'. The dew from the morning mist dripped from the beaten salt-pitted letters, like drops of rusty blood from the scars of aging time. The former sign of caution had become contrary and ironic to the fact that the gas-house was a common meeting place. Tales, stories, news of people, ships, the mainland, the world, would all be told, discussed and argued within the small stoking room of the gas-house. About thirty people could squeeze into the stoking room and most evenings the room was full. This was a time with no televisions, no radios, or telephones - most of the news was passed on by 'word of mouth' - most often by the mouth of Aonghas Sheórais the cobbler.

Aonghas would carryout the shoe repairs in the front window of his home. He could be seen walking the streets of Stornoway in the early morn carrying a large bag on his back which would accommodate the shoes to be delivered or collected for repair. His fingers were black and blue, bruised as a result of his work with hammer and shoe iron. Many a time people would laugh and shout at Aonghas, 'Yer fingers would nae be sae sore if ye' watched yer shoes instead o' the street'. Aonghas wore a cap which was badly burnt, especially at the front. The latter was the result of his sitting over a peat fire which was in the middle of his room, and nodding his head while half asleep. 'Ye' should go tae yer bed, sitting sleepin' and listenin' for news', was many the cry from a neighbour.

John waited, poised in his gateway. He was like a statue; still and silent, the only sign of life was the occasional puff of smoke from his old, black burnt pipe. Suddenly, his pipe gave a loud angry hiss as a solitary globule of red, rusty water dripped into the deep burning embers to instantly escape as a steamy spirit back to the mists from the fires of hell. Through the stillness of the early morn loomed the shadowy figure of Aonghas the cobbler walking toward the gates. The gas-house was always his first stopping place - the beginning of his round. Aonghas walked towards John slowly. People did not rush in Lewis, there was no need.

Aonghas was a tall, thin man and his long legs seemed to move with a slow, lurching stride, as if walking on thin ice which may give way at every step. John made his way back to the stoking room to open the furnace door - something he did every winter's morning so that Aonghas could 'have a warm'.

"Ah ah John, 'tis freezing today, freezing, what, what, what?" Aonghas had a habit (which some found very annoying) of ending most of his sentences with a barrage of what, what, what. Some believed this habit of speech to be derived from his trying to pry news from unsuspecting victims.

"Yer like a scavenging raven", was the common cry from Stornoway folk - a saying most likely originating from the unusual feature of his long, hooked nose. Aonghas stood with his back to the roaring furnace. "Ah, John what news, what news, what, what?"

"Nae news Aonghas, nae news", replied John, who was a

quiet, soft-spoken man. John removed two kippers which were hanging from a piece of string across the front on the furnace to warm. He placed each of the kippers upon a dark tin plate and handed one to Aonghas. The two sat on stools in front of the furnace as they slowly ate the kippers while occasionally spitting bones into the fire. Aonghas suddenly shouted out (as was his way), "Sad news, sad news, Barabel Nicaundra passed away, God bless her, sad news, 89 years, and such a kind old soul, sad news, what, what, what".

John replied, softly and slowly, "Ah, sad news, God bless her".

Aonghas continued, "I'll be asking old Macomerat when the funeral be". Old Macomerat was the grave digger.

They were interrupted by the sudden intruding sound of the shipyard's solitary haunting bell. It was 8 a.m. The toll of the bell summoned the shipyard workers. It was a time when there were few clocks and no watches. Each time the bell tolled was an indication to come or to go to work. John and Aonghas stood and tossed the remainder of their kipper bones into the roaring furnace. John wiped the kipper oil from the two tin plates with an old black cloth. Aonghas walked out of the stoking room with his characteristic long, lurching stride. "Ah, I'll be seein' ye' at the first noon toll, be news, be news, what, what". He disappeared down the road with his bag o' shoes, to complete his round tour of the town.

John stood at the gas-house gate with his foot trailing behind into the gas-house compound. Any strangers who may have passed by would have, at first glance, thought John to be trapped in the gas-house gate.

Soon the sounds from the shipyard invaded the silence. 'Twas like an orchestra to John's ears. The repetitive, deep, vibrating **thump, thump, thump** from the steam engine's massive piston - a tired and weary foundation without which little could be done. In opposition to the deep bass drum of the giant piston, was the high-pitched, ear-piercing screech of the saws from the shipyard mills. Occasionally there would be the long hissing sound of steam escaping from the engine's safety valve - like a giant dragon hissing in anger. What brought the orchestra to life was the multitude of ringing bells from different types and sizes of hammers. Some wooden mallets, some small, metal lump hammers and some mighty sledge hammers that only the strongest of men could swing for hours. Bang, tap, bump, thump, tap, and tap thump, hissssss, screeeech.

John smiled from the gas-house gate. Another day had begun in Stornoway and he was happy.

John walked swiftly back to the furnace to start shovelling coal to keep the fires burning. Old Wilson, the gas-house manager, was on his way, walking towards the stoking room. Old Wilson was about 68 years of age. Small, fat and round, he always had the smell of whiskey on his breath, and his nose was big, red and pot-holed, thus, his nic-name 'copper nose'. He was bossy and pompous and was feared by many, and, not liked by any. These were days when a job could be lost in an instant with no retribution. John had once overheard a dispute between 'copper nose' and a more educated worker from the gasworks.

"Yer sacked McLeod, get yer tools, and get ye' oot".

MacLeod had retorted very angrily, "Ye' old copper nosed bombastic drunkard".

John did not know the meaning of the word 'bombastic' but it had stuck in his mind and was always muttered as 'copper nose' approached. John could hear the sound of footsteps as he shovelled coal into the furnace, mumbling, 'Ye bombastic drunkard. Ye cursed bombastic - that's all ye be a bombastic'. Copper nose barged into the stoking room as if he owned it, "What be goin' on in here then?" Most workers never answered the manager. He would ask a question then answer it himself. "What be going on in here then? Nothing, ah! That meter gauge is too low! Why is it low? A talkin' and messin' about at the gate! Will ye be needin' more coal? Yes, more coal! An, an, what's that ye be mumbling man? Ah nothing! Now, is everythin' fine? Yes! Well take heed now, take heed". Copper nose shuffled out of the room to leave John angrily mumbling to himself, 'bombastic - bombastic drunkard - bombastic - bombastic - bombastic, he's nothing more than a bombastic, a pure bombastic'.

The bell tolled high noon. In an instant the giant orchestra from the shipyard became silent. 'Twas just as if a switch had been turned to 'off'. From the sudden silence came the clip, clop, clipity-clop of a pony's hooves upon the cobbles, as it pulled a cart full of coal towards the gas-house gate.

"Ah, hi John, how be ye'?"

"Ah, hi Tormod an Goha, I be a lot worse for seeing

'copper nose', he's a bombastic, nothing more than a bombastic".
Suddenly, Aonghas appeared, lurching along to the gate, "What, what, what news, what be a goin' on, what, what?"

John opened the gate for the pony and cart. The cart was backed-up against a hatch-way in the stoking room wall. The three men shovelled the coal from the cart into the room. When they had finished, Aonghas shouted so loudly he may have been heard at the shipyard, "Food lads! Food! What, what and news, news I have - what, what". The three men retired to the stoking room for food, rest and gossip.

John removed an old pan of black tea from a hot metal plate on the side of the furnace. There were four wooden cargo chests in the room and two stools. The three men each sat on a chest whilst using the other as a table. John had an old tin drum standing on bricks to one side of the furnace. He put a shovel full of hot coals from the furnace into the round tin drum which had holes punched into the bottom to let the air to the fire. "Now", said John, "Tatties and lobsters". He placed four large potatoes into the hot coals. Then a metal grid was placed over the top of the tin drum onto which was placed a large old gallon tin full of water. Once the water had come to the boil, John dropped three large lobsters into the liquid. At this time fish, crabs and lobsters were bountiful and a main part of the islanders' diet. John placed three of his oily tin plates onto the table and poured the black tea into three tin mugs from the old pan. He tipped the water from the lobsters and placed one onto each plate. John then removed the three baked tatties (potatoes) with a long pair of coal tongs and placed one next to each lobster. The people of Stornoway were skilled in the art of cooking and eating fish and shell fish. The three men broke into their lobster with a life time of experience. They ate heartily as they spoke of news from far and near, while tossing and spitting any waste shell from their lobsters into the furnace. "Ah", shouted Aonghas. The three men quickly filled their pipes. 'Twas like a ritual. The pipes would be lit and then the important news from Aonghas would be broadcast. The three men sat wide-eyed with expectation, sucking excitedly on their pipes. Aonghas turned his head to each side, looking over his shoulder to see if anyone was spying - going to steel his secret news. The latter was ironic as the news would be known by everyone in the town within hours. Aonghas, who always shouted loudly around the streets, now whispered his secrets. "News - be news, simple Sampson, the half-wit has disappeared, vanished into nothing, gone".

John and Tormod could hardly contain their excitement, "Ooo - ooo!"

Aonghas continued, "Aye - just disappeared he has, gone from the earth, and only God knows where. Most the town be looking for 'im and 'e be nowhere to be seen".

"Maybe he's fell down a well!" said John in a whisper.

"Or maybe he's fell in the sea", whispered Tormod.

Suddenly Aonghas took a hold of Tormod's wrist, "Ah listen to this". The latter action was an indication that the next piece of news would be eerie as Tormod was well known for the telling of ghost stories and frightening young children. Aonghas continued, "There were flashes of light seen by many last night over the Callanish Stones".

"Ooh, ooh" retorted Tormod who hastened to add, "That be the devil's work, the marching stones and the sleeping woman of the hills. I tell ye' 'tis the devil's work afoot".

Aonghas continued, "The clachair, the stone mason is still spending hours and days in 'is shed and dae ye' know what fir?"

John and Tormod leaned over towards Aonghas.

"He's in his shed". Aonghas again turned his head to each side to make sure his secret would not be stolen. "He's in his shed making his own tombstone".

"Ooh nae", replied John.

"There be something not holy about that", interrupted Tormod, planning another ghost story.

Aonghas carried on, "Captain James be back with yon 'Scottish Thistle'. He be back from Marseilles. He be sharing' a dram or two with Captain David. Bah! He's a mean man Captain David, I sat next to them at the inn and he shouted, 'be gone, be on yer way'".

John and Tormod started laughing. "Ha, ha, Captain David be knowin' what yer at ha ha", shouted John.

Aonghas took a hold of Tormod's wrist. Again this was the sign, the sign for an eerie tale, "Nancy Murray's ghostly voice was a heard to be singing on the winds of Loch Bhraon".

"Ooh, ooh", replied the audience.

Aonghas continued with his news, "Allan McMurchy and Rob

Macorachie were a fightin' over pretty Mary Shibbelag".

"Shame be on the two of them", shouted John.

"I've nae finished yet", shouted Aonghas across the tea chest table, "news, news, what, what, Natty the teacher, Callum MacAran the baker and Allister na Miaran, ye' know! Thimble Sandy the tailor. Something be afoot. The three of 'em were like three old hens a cackling' and whisperin' at the inn last night".

"Something afoot", whispered Tormod.

"News, news, wait 'til ye' hear this". Aonghas quickly peered over each shoulder, "Captain Jack Tar be back with the good ship 'Mercury'".

John interrupted, "Nae, nae, John McAllan left when he was a young lad".

Aonghas continued, "He was in church last Sunday, in the same seat where his initials J.M.A. were carved. Not a soul knew who he was". Aonghas took another quick glance over each shoulder before continuing, "Then suddenly after the service he walks over to his sister Peggie".

John was amazed, "Aye, aye, aye 'tis a strange world for sure, and I di'nae know what makes it turn".

"More news, what, what, those Maclachlans".

Tormod interrupted, "Arr they be sinners, sinners, what be with them?"

Aonghas whispered, "Henny - Henny was drunk and singing after midnight and went back with sailors and boarded the 'Mercury'".

"Sinful woe, sinful woe, may God forgive her", replied John sadly.

Aonghas said, "And I've nae finished yet, Henny's brother Daibhidh was at the side of the road lay down again, he was frothing at the mouth and people stood around watching. Then he stands up, all red in the face, with a bowed head, all ashamed, and walks away and decent people shouting after him, 'sinner, sinner'".

Tormod started to imagine a fine eerie tale as he added, "'Tis demon possession, aye demon possession. He does it regularly. The Maclachlans are possessed sinners, so they are".

"More news, more news", said Aonghas, "pretty Shonat McAulay from Suilavig was around at old Peggy Bean Ruari's house, aye, went to see her friend Aerig". "Something afoot, something afoot".

"Not much more news now", retorted Aonghas sadly,

"Ah, I remember now, old Callum has left the sawmill. He collapsed last Sunday at church, not a well man, poor Callum".
John and Tormod joined in, "Ah poor old Callum, a God-fearing man, God bless him".
Aonghas stopped talking and thought deeply, "Ah! Now, now, ah! I remember, Callum Phadrig, husband to Bellag Uistean is feared to be lost at sea".

"Ah, sad news, he was aboard the brig Arethusa, sad news", replied John sadly.

"**Ah**!" Aonghas jumped quickly and took a hold of Tormod's wrist which caused John and Tormod to jump in shock. "I near' forgot, one for you Tormod. Nighe Hespi, the witch, she crossed the path of old Callum when he was goin' a fishin'. And Callum was cursed, aye, caught no' a single crab or fish".

"Ooh, ooh", retorted the audience.
Tormod whispered, "There be things a do, things a do, Nighe Hespi was seen by children floating through the mist".
Suddenly, the bell tolled the return to work and the three men automatically stood up to return to their tasks.

John checked the gauges on the furnace and shovelled more coal into the hatch. At 3 p.m. John was sat outside smoking his pipe, as he often did. 'Twas a beautiful winter's day, fresh, sunny, with a calm sea. John sat looking over the harbour. The bell tolled for the half-hour, three o'clock workers' break. The shipyard became silent. John watched the water which was like a sheet of glass. He could see some sea lions heads peeping with big round eyes, waiting for fish scraps, often thrown from many a 'Zulu' wherrie returning from a fishing trip.

About ¼ of a mile out at sea could be seen the large black fin of a basking shark (harmless to people) like the sail of a small boat. An eagle circled overhead waiting to dart like a bullet at some unsuspecting prey. John started to fall asleep within the peace and bliss of the surrounding beauty. Suddenly, he jumped as his eyes beheld the full splendour of a mighty giant in front of him. 'Twas the barque 'Johannes Koser', with towering masts and full white flapping sails. As the ship sailed from the harbour, there was a hiss, like a snake, as the bows cut through the mirrored water like a knife. The massive sails occasionally flipped with a sound like a whip as they caught and tussled with a cold winter breeze. It was a majestic sight. Orders could be heard like an echo as the captain shouted loud and clear in his proud, deep voice of authority. 'Winch the main beam', and immediately there was the clicking sound of the metal cogs being hand wound by a sailor. As John watched the stern of the ship pass by he could see the faces of people staring and waving. A tear ran down his cheek. John remembered many years ago when his own son had sailed to America. He had received the occasional letter from his son, delivered by sailors passing through. His son was now married and they had a daughter whom John would most likely never see. John was now 69 years of age and the coal dust and pipe had taken its toll on his chest. The shrieking bell screamed out its haunting, angry, demanding sound. John returned to stoke the furnace - he felt sad - he wondered if he would ever see his family again.

Many a visitor called by the gas-house during the afternoon where news would be secretly whispered, to then be told to all. At 5 p.m. the bell tolled the end of a hard day's work. John swept the clay floor of the stoking room and threw the bits of coal, fish scraps and tobacco ash waste into the furnace. Each evening was busy at the gas-house. People would meet and often, they would all be squeezed into the room like herrings in a barrel. At 7 p.m. the gas-house room was crammed full of people. The air was thick with pipe smoke and all were excited about the evening's entertainment. The occasional bottle of rum was passed between the audience and the room was a hum with everybody talking and exchanging news. There were workers from the shipyard and the tweed mills, and young children laughing and squeezing between the adults. "Young Donald MacLeod, stop spitting on tae them hot coals, ya' dirty beast". The shout was followed by a 'clip around the ear' from the young offender's mother. He never repeated the crime again.

Tormod lightly touched the centre of a small black cross which was about four inches in length. The room instantly became silent. The cross was the signal - a sign that somebody was going to tell a tale. Every time a tale was about to start, the storyteller would touch the centre of the cross with their fingertip as if it offered some kind of protection. The cross was said to be invincible. It was made of some kind of black marble. Some said it was found hundreds of years ago at the Callanish Stones. Many tales surround the cross, yet invincible it seems to be as it has been with John's family and ancestors for as long as? nobody knows. Tormod removed his finger from the centre of the cross. He spoke softly through the silence, "There be a tale to be a telling and if ye' fear easy, be leavin' the room. The tale is of the flashing lights over the Callanish Stones seen last night". There was a fearful mumble around the room and John touched the centre of the cross once more as if extra protection was needed in the room. "This young man, a traveller to our shores will tell the entire tale". Tormod pointed towards a young man of about 25 years of age. The young man stepped forward and touched the centre of the cross with a trembling hand. The room was silent. Many a tale would be told each evening by many a different man or woman. The young man began to speak slowly and fearfully through the thick smoke in the room, and all knew this would be one of the haunting tales from the gas-house.

The following morning John was standing in the half open gas-house gateway as was his custom. He stared intensely along the road which led to the gas-house stoking room. It was misty, silent and still. Slowly, through the mist, walking towards John, a young boy appeared. John smiled - this was what he had been waiting for.

CALANAIS
The March of the Standing Stones

Hiking along, as I skip, the Highland beat,
Road, and path, and glen.
With arched and craning neck and back,
the scorching sun, in the highland hills,
stretching muscle, skin and bones to crack,
I sit to bathe my swollen feet,
in an ice-cool flowing, bubbling stream.
I gasp with pleasure and relief,
nature raw, beyond belief.

I had walked for miles,
backpack, creaking, squeaking, moaning,
to the beat of blistering feet,
No! I hop, skip and jump,
the pots and pans,
my one-man band.

Perchance upon a local inn,
a watering hole, a rest, some food.
A local yarn to spin.
I make merry, jest and drink a wee dram,
or two,
so many malts, 'tis untrue,
the mountain stream,
the heather's golden dew.

Succumb to local custom,
a simple English travelling man.
Tales of duns and brochs and Fir Bhréige,
false men and spirits,
stone clad, like standing stones,
old time, whispering Lew's folk,
Ah-l-oooo-ee! 'tis the fear of God in me.

I left the inn, Ah! the world does spin,
and the road does wag and weave.
The sun and moon, two eyes on me,
a haunting, hunting tease.
So late, and yet so light,
suddenly, how could the sunset dip so quick,
'tis the blanket of the night.
I know not where I be,
but I feel, within the silence,
something waits for me.

I start to climb, a long and forlorn hill.
The heather, wet, yet crisp, shhh! 'telltale',
my heart does pound and beat,
ghosts and spirits and standing stones,
Shhh! too much noise, the devil I may meet.

A misty moonlit night,
my head still spin.
Half asleep, I pull my blanket,
a cocoon of safety, I quickly clamber in.
The mist, so thick, so cool and fresh,
my eyes, so heavy, slowly flicker,
as a candle flame's last gasp of life and hope, deliver.
SUDDENLY! Icy breeze,
my body quiver,
as if deep in a frozen river.
From peace and rest, my heart burst in my chest,
I cannot breath, my stomach heave,
I try to sink into the earth,
lest my spirit, see, uncover,
a tale be a tale,
yet this I know be real.
This site I see,
it still haunts me,
it be like none other.
I silently roll, back into a furrow,
life or death, be seen,
I crave for life, tomorrow.

The mist does flicker,
playing with a moonlit breeze,
my eyes transfixed,
I dare not blink,
so silent breathe.
I see a line of standing ..... what?
Stone, or men, or spirits,
the moonlit night, and flickering mist must be.
And yet! They seem to march,
they seem to march - to me.
They turn and spin as people who,
who celebrate, a ritual feast.
Silver goblets catch the moon,
shimmering, with henbane,
I know something,
one thing will happen soon.

Hiding, I watch in fear and awe,
I pray to God for life,
I swear to sin no more.

Suddenly all movement stops,
I listen to a deep, low hum,
as if some meditating 'om'.

The figures slowly move,
to form a circle,
now, so clear, I see.
Their eyes closed tight,
their arms all raised,
all pointing, over me.

I wait, and wait, to turn my head,
to face, what?
For something,
one thing be.
My fingers claw the earth,
a hole to dig, escape,
to hide from fate,
a sacrifice,
my life, tonight, a key.
All so slowly, slowly, I move and turn,
every twitch of springing grass,
a thunderous blast,
my only hope for life,
keep secret,
Please God be with me tonight.

The hum, hum, humming,
vibrates and shakes,
so quiet and low,
and yet 'tis like,
an atomic blast, some miles away.
The mushroom,
you see last.

My wide and staring eyes cannot believe,
a lady sleeping upon the hills,
18, the moon, of change and chance,
love or lust, a wild romance,
so peaceful, waiting 18 years,
one night's sleep,
for something, one thing,
I pray my soul to keep.

The shimmering moon does dance,
floating, skimming, the dreaming lady of the hills.
Gliding, stroking, so gentle in the night.
A magic, secret, silver, white,
the moon, to swoon, so soon, be on her lips,
the moonlight kiss,
rising mist to clouds,
the breath of life,
reborn, wake from the night.

Moonshine, ley-line, earth-shine, time-line,
the lady of the hills,
turn white this night,
as if a blowing, gusty, gasp,
for life,
the swirling, breathing mists,
spiral high to rise,
for what, to see,
to kiss a star,
Capella,
the brightest star that be.

Riding on a chariot,
her beauty never sway,
Capella, as a shimmering pearl,
she rides the Milky Way.
I watch in awe and fear,
I listen to the deep hum, vibrating wheels,
the horses beating hooves,
coming down on me.

Panic, I rip myself free from my cocoon,
an insect waiting for the hawk,
the tearing beak,
to catch my soul,
I run to find a hole,
I run along a long broad ridge,
rising to Cnoc an Tursa,
6000 years now in the past,
each step may be my last.
The sound, deep hum, the chariot of fire,
chasing, coming after me.
What be my fate?
My very bones do quake,
running down a stoned avenue,
a corridor, to lead the prey, one-way,
the corner of one eye, I glimpse,
people digging with antlers and shoulder bones,
a grave for me?
'Tis grave to die this way.
Now into the centre of the stones,

I clamber, crawl, pure panic,
my back against a monolith,
as a grave stone black,
towering high, a sacrificial slab?

The chariot, pure white,
roaring down, Stone Avenue,
thunderous horses, beating hooves.
Suddenly, snorting white, cold steaming,
freezing breath upon my face,
so cold to burn,
a frost, white mist, to churn.

As a bolting animal, craving life,
I see a chambered Cairn,
Like a mouse to a hole, or trap,
I grasp for life,
like a piece of string,
from a mountain crag,
my body heavy drag.

I sit within my chambered Cairn,
my crypt, my tomb, death's womb.
Glittering arrowheads line the walls,
beautiful colours catch the light,
Quartz, xylonite, with shafts of silver pearl.
I see no bow, to make a fight,
I accept my fate, whatever be,
something, one thing be, this night.
Suddenly, silence, I press my back,
against my crypt,
as if to press a secret door,
No way. My eyes glance to the floor.

Lying on a bed of heather,
a warrior with sword in hand,
he looks as if some battle fought,
his blood stained clothes,
his cuts to bruise.
I wonder what the battle,
did he win, or lose.
Through wire, like heather beard,
he gasps short breaths for life,
as if to steal life from the air,
waiting for ..... something, One thing.

The warrior's hand drop from his hilt.
A deep man's groan of death,
the pain nay in the body, but with belief 'tis said,
"My sword, my sword",
I kneel beside this warrior man,
I can smell his sweat and blood,
I see his sword, with a thousand dints,
where blood did rip and drip.
I take his hand, 'tis like a giant mallet,
so heavy, lift onto the hilt.
"Bless you", says he,
And I reply, "Aye, God bless you".

Through the silence, faint sound of footsteps,
to invade our chambered Cairn,
I hold the warrior's hand, so tight,
as if in resurrection,
he may, rise to fight,
to save our lives this night.

Footsteps, gentle, enter the secret Cairn,
What monstrous death or fate awaits?
I pray the end be quick,
or will my body in endless pain,
be taken, bit by bit.

The dark Cairn, in an instant, light so bright.
I shade my eyes,
I feel a calm, no fright.
Stood in the archway to the Cairn,
beauty beyond any man's delight.

She stood so small,
so delicate and fragile,
so white, as if inside, beneath her skin,
there was the brightest light,
so young, so pure, so white,
her hair flowed forever down to the ground,
an endless white snow avalanche,
with ice-like crystals, white diamonds,
glittering and flickering,
a moonlit, starlight shimmering dance.
She need no clothes, she was dressed in light,
her eyes were like silver pearls,
pupils, tiny moons, so bright.
She touched my soul, my heart,
such beauty, painful, my body ache,
the feeble man to shake,
such beauty beyond a wildest dream.
My eyes drip tears,
I sigh and cry,
a pain of joy,
with no release,
I cry and cry,
Please,
No,
Something,
Something, one thing,
I should, this day, not know,
a mortal man, be borne upon,
be born again, the circle now bestow.

Dare I speak, yet I feel no fear,
but a tormented atmosphere,
as if a search be here.
Still kneeling by my warrior friend,
I hold his hand, so heavy upon his hilt.
His sword to grasp, like life, within the light,
his eyes did flicker, still.
The warrior mumbles deeply,
staring now at the light,
"Who are you?"
The Goddess replied, "Selene", and
walked towards the dying warrior,
to kneel beside his side.
She took his other hand in hers,
she spoke, and then she cried,
"Endymion, Endymion, is it you?"

A spectator in awe, I watched.
I can see the sadness in your eyes,
as 18 years pass by,
one day to you,
to change all time,
the tears for pain, too few.
Endymion, who waits and sleeps,
the gift eternal life and youth,
eternal sleep, the thief.
The Gods' move in mysterious ways,
beauty's eternal grief.

Selene's voice, so sweet, like a song,
"Endymion, Endymion, is it you?"
She bent and gently kissed the warrior's lips,
his last gasp pure delight.
I saw his spirit rise and fly,
a butterfly, so free,
into an endless night.

Selene cried and cried her tears,
of burning ice,
to turn to charcoal, body and ground,
I fear again this night.
She stared into my eyes,
she put her face so close,
"Endymion, Endymion, is it you?"
She kissed my lips, I close my eyes,
my very soul did shake.
A taste so sweet, no man could know,
my legs so weak,
please, last forever, never go.
She moves away, I fall down to the floor,
my soul can stand no more.

Selene sobs and gently turns,
she steps so lightly from the Cairn,
a crypt to die,
return, rebirth,
the moon of change,
The galloping chariot rage,
and all of time refrain.

The lady sleeps, now,
in the hills, go see,
the stones, the circle, and the cairn,
frozen, tears of time,
No beginning, be no end,
monoliths, stone, cold, bones,
until, fulfil,
The march of the standing stones.

THE CLACHAIR

A taciturn man, stonemason.
Walking, eyes downcast, what words?
Carved in stone? What thoughts?
Short and bowed with age and time,
Living in a house known as the Ark.
In an old boat wreck
down beneath the deck,
through a wooden door, with a black iron sneck.

A thick impervious floor of oak,
portholes, escape, the peat fire smoke.
Small and multifarious life's contents,
carved stones and rock, statues,
so delicately hewed, with chisel and mallet,
ships, galleons, stags, sheep and cattle,
Secrets, all hidden within stone block,
such delicate, giant hands to wrasse.

Spare and sparse the arching walls,
beneath the deck,
like Jonah in the belly of a whale.
Old timbers, splintered, cracked, prevail,
woodworm mottled, dappled, flecked,
Piebald, speckled, stippled, bereft,
trapped in time, aching timber, oak and pine,
The old 'Gun-Brig', pose, appeasing time,
proud masts still tall, bear the old clothes line.

A rusty cutlass and an old flint lock,
past wars, encounters, skirmishes and frays,
nought now, be peace, repose, long days
chip, chip away, some secret?
while the pendulum swinging sways.

An out-back shed of bracken and wood,
The clachair sits on an old tin tub.
Chip-chipity-chip, the mallet tap,
chisel, sculpting, engrave, the final chafe.
For months, hands plying, chisels hone,
intent, create, one's own tombstone.

Black marble, sandstone, pink or buff,
a living man, his death to bluff?
or to survive, immortality? Ah! what words,
some miraculous chant, or magic verse?
To stare each day, death in the face.
The tombstone's humble silence,
saved for a lonely wake.

Born " " ". Died " " "?
To face, or guess, the final date,
to dig one's grave, by the old church gate,
why live to plan the grave,
is life too long, be death too short,
'tis a hidden path all have to walk.

Maybe, a seer see, some oracle?
to know, sibyl, whispering lips, siren's yell.
Cold, black, hole in the earth. A wishing well.

The children sneak, to peep,
curiosity, adventure, risk, and danger,
secrets for the gas-house tales,
furtive, windows, curtains, veils.

The two boys creep, so silently,
The clachair sleeps this night,
a snoring growl from the earth bound wreck,
twilight, by a ship of death.

Creep, creep, the secret mission,
for the island now to save,
what be? the chipping noise once heard,
a message for a dead man's grave.
Ah! Maybe some secret news, news,
Tormaid - what, what, to pay a price
Ooh! some coins for cakes and sweets,
Ooh! that would be nice.

Creep, creep, creeping, so silently, the giant sleeps tonight.
Be darker now, yet the moonlight shines so bright.
Shh-shh, the heart beat deep,
up to the window, creep, creep, creep.

Stand on tip-toe, look in window,
Aww! The tombstone shape,
a monolith, shining in the twilight, glisten,
like a giant gateway. SUDDENLY
AWWWW, AWWWW, the boys
fall with a piercing scream.
A devil's head, black, horns, red eyes,
screeching, like the banshee cry's.

The two boys in an instant gone,
two warriors forlorn, Callum and Ian,
purring, licking paws, in the window, sat.
'Tis, the clachair's big fat hairy, black tom cat.

Aged with time the clachair,
walks the moonlit night,
his fishing boat to row from shore,
through mists of life, and forlorn strife.
Callum and Ian, curiosity, nae killed the cat,
teenagers now, the mind still wonders,
what, when, why, some secret, sigh.

Behind the sand dunes, watching,
the clachair rows into the mist,
Ahhh - what be now, the two lads scream,
slowly, through the mists, towering,
masts and sails, St. Elmo's Fire.
Ghost ship, white sails, flickering, silver, silky veils,
"The clachair sails tonight" cries Ian.

The ship turns tail in flight,
into the night and northern lights,
with licking, kissing, flames of glory
and sounds of sailors singing on the wind,
sailing in a line through time,
to find the start, where the end begin,
and the circle nae decline.

Ho - Ho sailor lads
sail the deep blue sea,
by the tides of time
Yo! we sing a rhyme
tag the ropes
let the main sail free.

Ho - Ho sailor lads
kiss the salt, spit the rum, be free,
by the tides of time
Yo! we sing a rhyme
tag the ropes
let the anchor free.

The song, the clachair and the ghost ship
disappeared into swirling mists,
Callum and Ian stared at each other
mouths wide open, and a long time be,
before the two did rise, rise to see.

Both lads nae spoke, yet both lads knew,
now the time to see within,
the bracken shed, the clachair dead,
what words, be the tombstone, said.

Both lads still shook with fear,
some memories ever last,
as they opened up the shed door,
the devil screamed as black tom cat, shot past.

The two crept up to the old tombstone,
mouths aghast, in awe,
neither two could nae believe,
could not believe what they both saw.

On the dark blue-green shiny marble,
was ????

Upon the dark blue-green, shiny marble
glittering like an endless sea.
Was the ghost ship carved
with shimmering sails, and sailing, oh so free.
And as clearly as can be,
waving, standing, staring, with a bottle of gin,
stood the clachair
with a sly old grin.

NIGHE HESPI

The witch! Her house a hovel
surrounded by water, slime and ducks,
familiars, chickens, cats and mice,
bent and ancient, wrapped in shawl,
nae tae be seen in the old church hall.

The hens would chant, a coquettish pose,
listening with intent, as only hens may do,
as she chattered, a chirping chant,
be spells, a curse on you.
Feeding mice, with given names,
the cats do sit and stare,
as if their nature be subdued,
their souls turned out, thread bear.

'Tis said Nighe Hespi makes effigies
from peat and bones, with heather hair,
to put o'er fire, 'tis many the fever came from there,
with pins to stick and sticks to poke
'twas many who had a swollen throat.

One way, the grain, in line, the river flow.
Independence, difference, deviation, diversity,
eradicate, exterminate, disintegrate, annihilate,
rack, fire, ducking stool, pointed tool
beware the spoken rules and laws, Nighe Hespi
for superstition, do's and don'ts, will's and won'ts.

If Nighe Hespi cross your path,
bad luck, on you, befall, if you believe,
nae fish today for Callum, nought but old seaweed.
And children listen, fear and learn,
evil deeds, to rid the evil witch.
Imagination, fired by adult tales.
To tempt the devil, 'knock a door and run',
to tease and taunt, why not? be she condemned.
To torture, temper, be in the end, amend.

Often, Nighe Hespi walks upon the shore
collecting driftwood, for her fire.
One sea-fresh misty day some children play,
playing in the sand upon the beach.
Through the mists Hespi appears,
with ghostly driftwood, drifting
like a spirit ever shifting.
Revenge be sweet "oooo-oooo" cries Hespi,
to the children's quick retreat.
"Ahh-ahh 'tis Nighe Hespi, the witch,
we be cursed, to evil fate".

When Hespi died, no soul cried,
she be buried in a wayward grave,
alone, to rest in peace, a spirit free,
she wanders misty shores, to laugh with glee,
as children run and scream with fear,
"Ooo-ooo Nighe Hespi's ghost be here".

ZULU

Howling wind, cliff face, blasting rocks
the sea below explodes
like a raging barrage of bombs and shells.
Surely hell could be no worse,
the devil be wild this day, a curse.

She stands and waits, at the Port of Ness,
within an archway, made of rocks,
as if God knew, and made a tiny cave,
as if fate foretold, a sailor's wife,
to fear, her husband's unknown grave.

Within the endless, blackness, like a star,
a beautiful white face, with staring open eyes,
tears unseen, mixed the sea salt sprays,
her pale lips seem to tremble, to tremble as she prays.

Black clouds advance from the west,
swirling, endless depths, of bellowing fury,
clashing thunder, the young woman covers her ears in fear,
blinding lightning ripping all, the master Thor in glory.

Crashing waves, the cruel claw clutching,
to grab for any life, the sea in raging pain,
waves roll back, then come again,
a mighty blast, from flat cliff face, to sky, to howl,
exploding, white, spray, greeting clouds,
partners, one, deaths deep black cowl.

Zulu sails for home this night,
what choice? No choice, one choice, to fight.
Four men, weighted down to deck,
with hip-length, iron-shod boots and oilskins.
Neptune restless be, deciding fate, the ice wind spins.

Spindrift, the bucking decks awash,
pitch darkness, four men work, a fight for life,
"Let go" the hauling straining halyard,
"Hug to chest" from cleat, through swallow,
"Hands clear" the four-sheaved heavy block
"Whip lash" the steel wire hawser to yard.
Sail on you Zulu, Muirneag, wherrie,
"Spit salt" sea wash blood and blister,
"Finger lost", body torn, damn this frozen Minch,
deep beneath the soul, so free, the brave nae flinch.

Lightning flash, deep into dark, "see"!
A guiding star so bright.
The four men stare into the black of night,
a loving wife, an angel's face, a saviour, delight.

Sixty foot, the towering Zulu, pyramid sail,
sea to bash, gale to wail,
to dock at Ness, to home, to love, to wife,
to have a dram by the peat fire light.
You Zulu Warrior
to live, to sail, to sea, to fight.

THE COLL RIVER SILVER FISH DANCE

'Twas on the flat and sandy shore
of Old Broad Bay
by the mouth of the river Coll,
I lay one night by a peat fire light,
with a full moon, shining, round and bright.

'Twas as if the fish, were set to meet,
upon the shores of Long Island,
on the soft, wet, sandy beach.
fishes, silver streaks on a silver bed
the crabs and lobsters standing proud, and glistening, crimson red.

Small fish, large fish, star fish, Cray fish,
the prancing porpoise two by two,
to meet, the chance for true romance,
'twas the fishes silver moonlit dance.

The great night, on the shores
of Old Broad Bay,
the fish did flip and dance and sway,
the everlasting night away.
'Twas as if the sea, did bubble, and boil,
as a shimmering silver, diamond foil.
Crabs and lobsters, weaving and waving high,
as a Spanish dancer, clicking
claws, like fingers in the sky.

A little Lewis barefoot boy,
played his fiddle on the rocks,
like a magic whistling wind through caves,
from a hissing whisper,
to a howling scream,
fish spun wild, while silver eels,
jumped high into the black night sky,
to flash like lightening,
caught within the moon's unblinking eye.
The boy did play 'til his fingers bled,
and I would swear, he could play no more,
'twas like the music of the waves,
the waves to kiss the shore.

Thousands of fish, in the bright moonbeams,
like spotlights, at a ball,
dancing and spinning the night away
like starlit diamonds glittering bright.
I thought, no more could be this night,
then, the salmon and the sea trout did arrive,
to do, the Salty Sea Fish Jive.

I would not believe, if I had not seen
what I saw, was but all, by chance,
I finished my dram, to dream my dream,
'twas, the Coll River, Silver Fish Dance.

THE TALE OF THE LEWIS CHESSMEN

(Warning - do not read late at night)
Behold, Be Bold, Be Told,
A tale of death, murder, treachery.
Ah! Shall I? Yes! The tale unfold.

Wanderer, a hiking man I be.
One late evening, cold, mist, rain,
I see a cave, light sticks to fire,
a rich man, bread, butter and tea.
A misty eve at Uig,
my blanket so comfortable and warm,
I see a figure, a shadow,
in the cave's arched, open door,
"Ay -Ay there" was the cry,
"Come in" cries I.
A sailor boy came into the cave,
And sat down facing me.
He shook my hand and gently smiled.
We spoke, as we shared some tea.

He asked if I had found a bag,
Nought of which I knew.
He gently smiled, yet looked so sad.
He told a tale,
'tis a tale from the sailor lad.

The tale does start, at Ard Mhór,
beyond the mountains of Uig,
Where cattle grazed, on Loch Hamnavay,
and the herdsman was the Red Gillie,
Gillie Ruadh, climbed to the top
of Ardmore.
Behold, a ship riding at anchor, far below.
Red Gillie, a suspicious man,
he lay in wait, to see what be the fate.
Moonrise, a dark and misty night,
and through the lapping waters
silent creep, a small boat,
oars kissing circles, upon the water deep.
A young sailor boy, did meet the land

at Gleann-na-Curach.
Red Gillie watched, like hawk to prey,
the sailor boy's 'bag o' swag',
a secret come Red Gillie's way.

Red Gillie stalked the boy, to meet at Guire,
and the boy, was much, confused.
He knew not where he was nor why,
but had stole a lot, from the ship in dock,
and such a crime, be not forgot.

The captain's playthings in a bag,
a treasure be, that day.
A simple sailor boy, took flight,
to disappear in a cold and lonely,
deep, black, night.
Red Gillie, killed the boy,
temptation, lust, desire.
Who would know? For the boy did go,
as a thief, and an evil liar.

The body and his treasure hid,
Red Gillie headed home.
He told his master Calum,
there be a boat, in the loch, in dock,
let's take some men and plunder
then sink her bows, way under,
to sing, then dance,
to drink to chance.
The devil will rant
a sin, no one, will wonder.

Master Calum, a righteous man of God
banished Gillie from Balnacliffe.
The treasure be lost in the Uig sands,
near the sailors bones, that rot.
The Lord moves in mysterious ways,
His justice to begot.

Red Gillie, caught in Stornoway
for a multitude of crimes.
His nature be, for the hanging tree,
for Lord Kintail and Gallows Hill
opposite the ancient stronghold
of the old Siol Torquil.

Many years passed by, and the days be still,
as Malcolm MacLeod stood with his long-horned cows,
on a lonely heather hill.

As if some unknown, fate or spirit,
restless be, the sailor boy?
Killed in a frenzied spree,
a secret to unfold
the truth be told
of a wondering restless spirit forever roam
the sands and seas of everlasting time,
time locked, Pandora's box, a murder and a crime.

The old cow, rubbed upon the sand,
and dug her horns in deep,
an old bag fell upon the land,
and a whistling wind blew dust
across the ragged peat.
MacLeod stood frozen to the spot
as he saw the chessmen drop.

What be? Some effigy, some graven images,
such of the like, be never seen.
Malcolm MacLeod dropped to his knees
to pray, to God, for maybe, these the devils tools.
'Twas an eerie wind, so suddenly
to twirl around, a howling sound.
Malcolm cried out aloud, "Oh Lord, please Lord, save me",
and the cow did screech, a wail,
as, the like of, never known,
and the only thought in Malcolm's mind
was to be, now safe at home.
Suddenly, what was? An, an, apparition.
Malcolm's body did shiver, and his bones did shake,
a fear felt, never before.
'Twas a, a, sailor boy, stood by the bellowing cow,
pointing hand, to secret bag,
now lying clearly upon the sand
with a strap, to the cow's horn snag.

Suddenly, the cow did bolt and rear and roar,
the simple beast, could take no more,
and with bag dangling from one horn
to Malcolm ran
as if, a desert, whirlwind storm.

Ahhhh - Ahhhh - Malcolm ran, so fast,
so fast, a trail be left forever, now within the sand
they say, scorched brown upon the land.

Once home, Malcolm did drink much rum,
'tis said he did not speak
for many weeks
he drank and lay in bed,
as if a curse be in his head.

Time on, a gentleman from Stornoway
heard of this ghastly tale
and went with many men to see,
to see, what be, what may prevail.

They were to find, eighty chessmen,
which they took to Stornoway
and placed into museums at London and Edinburgh
where they remain unto this day,
and Malcolm MacLeod
received thirty pounds
to help to drink his fears away.

But please, sit tight, for the tale,
be more, or go now if you fear,
for what to tell, I tell you now,
a secret be, which no one, now, should hear.

Many years pass by and nought amend.
'Twas one wild, freezing winters day
when Rev. A. J. MacKenzie, with a friend
were exploring Ardmore.
"Best let be, MacKenzie",
spoke wisely so, his friend.
They poked the sand with sticks
as if to find some secret clue,
maybe a coven, be a witch,
maybe a secret hole,
curiosity, what was it be, to fear MacLeod
to chill his very soul.

Three hundred years, yet some things
Time nae change.

"Best let be, MacKenzie, head for home,
I feel a breeze,
be cold like ice,
within my soul, a stabbing, cold steel, knife".

The breeze turn to a gale of ice,
to push both men into a cave,
a cave so cold,
it felt as if a grave of old.

The two men sat within the cave,
awaiting for the storm to pass,
and yet could see a calm, beyond the wind,
beyond the wind a stillness be,
it was so still, the grass.
Both men shivered to the bone
yet both men were deeply stirred,
for something in the wind, was said,
it was a hidden word.

Suddenly, a pouncing fear,
a heart beat, hard, the breath a hiss,
to break free through the ribs,
as if the heart beat, true, to know,
to know a devil's kiss.

Both men sat within the cave,
frozen, staring, wide-eyed,
white-haired, like ghosts.
If you had been and seen the two,
you would have screamed and ran from hell
be a tale, be nought to boast.

Suddenly, faintly, slowly, as if a mist,
over a pile of stacked stones,
an apparition began to appear,
the wind did whistle *oooooo*.
and the men were froze in fear.
A sailor boy stood upon the rocks,
the blood ran from his head.
He kicked the rocks beneath his feet,
and there below
behold the bones, the bones of one man dead.
Both men did scream, and run,
like two lost souls from hell,
with snow-white frozen hair, spiked icicles,
wide mouths and eyes,
like living dead, from a cold death bed,
they both ran for their lives.

And now the secret be released,
so free, the soul, the sailor boy,
and yet, his spirit, be seen, but now and then,
as he wanders o'er the land,
forever to search for the Lewis Chessmen,
his treasure all so grand.

DÙNAN

Ghost blue boat, towering white sail,
creeping in, on velvet patchwork purple tide.
A secret whisper, on gentle breeze,
pursed lips, blow the dust reveal.
Sunlight, quickly hide, blankets of sleeping hills.
The giant sail, flip, flicker white,
fragile, moth, to find a light.

Autumn, Carloway, bathing, soundless, twilight.
Past, Kirivick, Dùnan, Little fort now gone,
for pier, with busy creaking, aching, block and tackle,
Capston clicking, the busy world perceive
with hand in glove, gold and silver dust, rainbow, lust.

Dùnan be eerie and deserted.
The lamp be lit upon the pier,
to greet lonely boats at night.
Across Loch Roag, past lichened rocks by Rothasgeir,
from Great Bernera
Ghost white boat, through mist appear.

Suddenly within the seas of silence
there was cried aloud an everlasting name,
Culrigrein, back-to-the-sun,
Iain, Iain, Bhàin.

SIMPLE SAMPSON SIMPSON, TINY PIPER SMITHY AND SHIFTY JACK PERKINS

This story begins in England,
London docks, around the time of 1830.
The hustle and bustle at London quays
with cobbled roads and horses belching steam.

Many a mighty schooner, ship or speedy clipper,
would squeeze and queue, be sardine or the kipper,
barrels would roll, rumbling thunder,
men would shout and look to sea in awe and endless wonder.

Poverty, hunger, and may be chance,
chance of wealth from distant shores,
to sail the seas, Cape Horn! The Bounty!
Secret isles, countless women and treasures,
Ay! to leave London's rat infested,
dirty, black, plagued Thames River,
where the city's sewage flows so free,
Ay! to have, a dream,
to take a chance, an opportunity at sea.

The fastest clipper upon the seas,
the Royal Hawk, set sail at dawn,
from London docks, to Scotland's Stornoway.
With four masts heaving sails
with blistered hands the rope be winched
Ay! Ay! proud Captain Starch, who never flinched.

The bows did heave, and
the stern did swell
young sailor lads, riding the waves,
be a secret wish, to quell.

Sea mates, sharing hopes and dreams
of treasures, distant lands,
rife, rumours from the dock side taverns,
of magic worlds
and endless gold-filled caverns.
Captain Starch had sailed the seven seas

to many continents to the lands of kings and queens,
"Ay! lads", three sailor boys unease
"me stomach aches, from biscuit, gravy,
an' salty fish, while the captain,
dines, his exotic dish".
Piper Smith be 22 years of age,
an engineer, the best, with steam and gears,
Smithy ducking flywheels
squeezing between the greasy cogs
his hands so black from old oil drops.

The rich be rich, and
the poor be poor,
yet sometimes, even trodden dogs
may try to even up the score.
three sailor lads with hopes and dreams
with blistered hands
from the ropes and endless, towering beams.

Simple Sampson Simpson was a simple lad,
seven feet tall, a solid brick wall,
doing four men's work the ropes to tug and grab,
23 years old he could not speak
yet would mumble endless chants
which turned around inside his head
within simple thoughts be hidden depths
a macabre fascination, Sam had with death.
"Tug o' the rope, breach the beam,
the dead be dead to sleep
at the bottom of the deep blue sea
alone with crabs
will death come back for me".

And so Simple Sampson Simpson
would mumble in a distant daze
for hours, over and over again
until a different chant
with a common death slant
in his mind would surely reign.
And only one man ever stood his ground
in a Simple Sampson fight

and he must have slashed be twenty times
at Sampson with a bowie knife
as Sampson stood in a pool of blood
and chanted for his life.

"If I die I sleep
tell me when I'm dead
is death to come for me
am I dying now to go o'er the bow
with the fishes beneath the sea".

Simple Sampson suddenly,
slowly and gently, placed one giant hand
around the angry, knife slashing sailor's throat
and gently squeezed, another chant
to the sound of breaking bones.

"Death nae came to see me,
tell me what you see
go swim now and hurry back
from the bottom of an endless sea".

No sailor ever crossed Simple Sampson
beyond that infamous day
and he was always given a stern wide berth,
Ay! a man that no man mars
as he stood in the sun without his shirt
a giant disfigured with scars.

Tiny Jack Perkins was shrewd and cunning, only 17 years old
his fingers were light and very nifty
and through the shadows of the night
he moved like a ghost, very shifty.
many a sailor awoke to find
some coin or trinket, left the mind,
"Was it last night's rum?
My ruby ring be gone?"
"The cards I played?
I lost my silver blade?"
"My old ma's cross?
Dam! must in the sea be lost?"

An' no man dare take Jack to count or task,
for his friend be Simple Sampson
with hands like spades, to dig men's graves
and in his shadow, the wise man be afraid.
So there be three friends
and none be closer
as each one's need be needed by t'other.
Tiny Jack and Simple Sampson Simpson need the brains
of Piper Smith.
Tiny Jack and Piper Smith need the strength and brawn
of Sampson's scorn.
And Tiny Jack with his artful craft
provided goods, food and drink for all.

Tiny shifty Jack, in the shadow of the night,
creeping through cabins and decks
like a tiny mouse, looking for?
some hidden need to feed.
Escape, from poverty, to wealth,
some treasured gift, a countless cost,
the danger and the risk.
To take a chance, to risk one's life,
the pounding heart's excitement,
beware the gleaming knife.

Just a bit of old Ted's rum.
Just a bit of Toby's tobacco.
Just a bit of ......oh! a silver ring.
Just a bit of shhh - Bobby's boiled sweets
and oh! no, no, no? the captain's cabin.

Tiny Jack stood in awe, at the captain's door.
The risk, to chance, of life or death,
to be rich or, to stretch the neck,
"Well!" whispered Jack,
"one peep will do no harm".
Within the captain's cabin,
loud snoring, "AH!" the treasures for Aladdin.
"Be quick", whispered Jack,
so many treasures from distant lands,
for Jack's aching, roaming fingers, too much, to be, at hand.
"Ah! What be this? Carved chessmen,
must be enough booty t' make me rich".
Tiny Jack pulled out his hidden canvas bag,
"Shh - shh be quick - be quick".
Whispering, shifty Tiny Jack Perkins,
"I must be quick, dawn's breaking".

Tiny Jack rushed back to his cabin
where Smithy and Sampson lay asleep.
"Wake up - wake up, you two, be quick!"

Tiny Jack	*Sampson*	*Smithy*
Wake up!	ooh	what be?
help me	ooh	what be?
be quick or I die,	a death	what now?
help me, or my neck'll stretch	to die	you silly bugger!
some chessmen	be death	what's in the bag?
Quick! To shore, to hide	death comes	you bloody fool!
Keep watch, lower me	to death	you'll be the death
to the row boat	to die	for us all
lower me down	down to die	we'll hang for this
I'll bury the loot	dig a grave	be quick!
I'll be back in a mo'	I can see	you fool!
from dark shadows	death waiting	you fool!

The Royal Hawk be anchored
at a Scottish Highlands Isle
as Tiny Jack rows hard, his boat
he wears a shifty smile.
Through the faint daylight
to a sandy bank
to dig and hide his loot.
"Ah!" Jack hears a noise
to interrupt his ploy,
an approaching steadfast boot.

Red Gillie	*Tiny Jack*
What be doing lad?	Nothing sir
this be private land	I be going now
What be? That bag?	Nae, nothing sir
Give me the bag	no, no, no,
Ah! Some treasured loot	'tis mine
'Tis death you meet tonight	Ahhh - Sampson.

The knife was sharp and quick
across the throat of Tiny Jack
and Sampson was not there to help
yet Sampson knew that Jack would not come back.
Red Gillie buried Tiny Jack,
and buried the chessmen too,
a thief to catch a thief at work
Jack's luck be the devil's brew.

Sampson and Smithy waited for the hour,
be long with sweat, as they could feel
the hangman's noose pull tight around their necks,
whispering and waiting.

Sampson	*Smithy*
Death be there	where be Jack
to dig a grave	far from sight
be in the ground	I cannot see him
to be so far from sight	'tis a bad fate woe this night
death gone now	come we must go
gone home for tonight	we know nought of this night.
To be so far from sight	remember Sampson

We know nought of this night.

Suddenly, cutting the silent
morning's misty air
the captain's shout, "**thief - thief - thief**
there be a thief about".
All hands rise with fear to meet the morn,
stood fast in a taught, tense line
to face, be dreaded, captain Starch's scorn.

The captain's rage no man has seen afore,
"I be visited this night by a skulking thief,
and I swear his neck will stretch,
I swear he will beg for his body to be
swinging high from the gallows
afore we dock at London.
Bosun! take stock, count the heads".
"There be one man down sir".
"And who pray that man be Bosun?"
"It be Jack Perkins sir,
And there be one boat a missin'".

The captain raged like thunder,
stomping, stamping, up and down the straight crew line,
and all hands thought the deck would crack
and each man thought the day his last.

"Dirty, thieving scum, scum from the devil".
The captain hung his head in shame
for such an affront, to an officer's pride,
he felt he only, his self to blame,
his self to stop temptations game.

"Now here this, this shameful deed
be done and gone. I will not have it known,
that one of my crew would affront me so.
But all you men will suffer
there be no kind hand, to be, discipline to know,
Sampson and Smithy, you be Perkins' ship mates?
Have you a hand in this treachery?
If so you will kiss death's gates".

Smithy shouted clear and loud,
"No sir, I know nought of this evil deed".
Sampson chanted to the crowd,
as Smithy felt his neck begin to stretch,
his life be on the line,
his body numb, the fear to feel
what would Sampson's chant reveal?
Sampson's voice did tremble, as a little boy's.
"I be not to go to kiss death's gates,
I done no wrong.
Jack be dead, and buried in the ground,
asleep with worms without a sound
he gone into the deep, dark night
to meet with death and a shiny knife

I be not to g..........".

The captain raged,
"Be silent you mumbling imbecile,
Bosun! those two mates of the thief,
they can kiss the gunners daughter,
50 lashes each"
"AY - AY sir".

Sampson and Smithy were laid and tied,
over the ship's gun barrel.
The crew stood in fear of the captain's wrath,
as blood did splash from the nine-tailed cat,
and Sampson's chant was in time with the lash,
"Whip - whip - whip
am I - at the - gates of death?
Whip - whip - whip
to sleep beneath - the earth - or sea
whip - whip - whip
whip me - 'til be - death - I see"

The crack o' the whip an' Sampson's chant
swirled with an echo through the silent morn
and filled the crew with dread and scorn
for it be Sampson's and Smithy's mate
who bestowed upon the crew
the dreaded captain's hate.

Sampson and Smithy were made to swab and scrub
the deck from bow to stern
and all the crew were put to task.
"Let no man rest until our return to London".
The captain screamed, "And at Stornoway
no man shall leave for shore
to merriment, rum or Scottish maid,
unless I know for sure
Jack Perkins be dead, deep in a grave".

This was bad news indeed.
At Sampson and Smithy, the crew
did snarl and spit and glare,
and all hands blades were gleaming bright
as the Royal Hawk docked in Stornoway
and Smithy knew that none would sleep that night.

At the midnight hour, the ship did lay at rest
in wait for the morn when captain Starch
would go ashore to obey the king's request,
for tweed and special salted fish
and to return with tartan Scots, who dance on swords
to screeching pipes, this was the king's own word.

At 1 a.m., the silent night was torn asunder
to the sounds of men as if at war
be souls and death to plunder.

At least ten men, like cunning, creeping cats,
had pounced with knives, upon the two,
revenge, to kill and take to task.
And captain Starch and the Bosuns
knew all, and stayed at ease, did hide
for someone had to pay with blood
for the theft of the captain's pride.

Sampson roared like a mighty lion, King Kong
and stood as strong as an old oak tree,
as knives did stab and slash and cut
yet, ten men died from Sampson's touch,
and as he calmly laid each man to rest
'twas as if he was gently, to ease a child to bed.
Smithy's blood ran cold, as he hid within
the cabin's hold,
as arms and bones did gently crack
each man, to be so calmly laid upon their back,
and all the time, Sampson's gentle chant
as if to a child, a gift to grant,
to sleep, within a dream, as if,
each man's last gasp, from the breath of life be,
to meet the gift of death to rest
to sleep, with peace to solve
Sampson's eternal quest.
"Lay ye down to rest in peace,
be still, be death t' meet
an' tell him soon t' come for me
can ya see him as ya sleep?"
Soon the cabin returned to silence

and all that be, to remain of life
was Sampson's eerie, gentle, whispering chant,
as each of the dead men's brows
were stroked like sleeping children,
be the death of a still-born night.
"Lay ye down to rest in peace,
be still, be death t' meet
an' tell him soon t' come for me
can ya see him as ya sleep?"

"Come on Sam", cried Smithy,
"I be no more on this cussed ship
'tis for our lives we flee",
to which Sampson started to chant,
"Lives to live or death ......"
"Shut up!" cried Smithy,
"run or stay, I be jumpin' ship
jumpin' ship to Stornoway".
Sampson again began a chant,
"I stay t' meet with death
t' meet wi' ...."
"Listen", cried Smithy who had a need for Sampson,
"come with me, I know where death is".
Sampson started to chant,
"At last I go t' meet with death
t' rest ....".

The two men quickly walked the streets
of Stornoway, the peace to mar
as Sampson lumbered dripping blood
and whispering chants
a simple mind, with depths so deep
the spirit be, for souls to meet,
the secrets of the night bequeath.

"Ah!" whispered Smithy,
"the shipyard! come on Sampson".
The two squeezed through
two towering gates, the ghostly silence to invade
there be no need to lock or bolt
for the gallows crime persuade.

2 a.m. creeping through the shipyard gates,
SUDDENLY —— **'DONG'**
Sampson clanged the shipyard bell
A piercing sound to wake
The dead from hell.

"You stupid bugger Sam, quick, run".

The two men ran into the sawmill
and hid beneath the sawdust mound
to hold their breath without a sound.
'Twas not long before, the two, asleep
did deeply snore, in the deep dust heap.

At sunrise, captain Starch called for the bosun,
"What be the commotion in the night bosun?"
"Ten men down sir and two maties of the
thief jumped ship".
The captain spoke softly to the bosun
from within his quarters.
"A bad bunch this crew, a bad bunch.
Well! that's what happens when captain Starch
is crossed, damned vagabonds, vagabonds.
Pick 12 hands from Stornoway,
they be good sailors and honest men,
but drill 'em well bosun, discipline!
and it'll be no more to do or spoken
of the breach of my quarters.
Let it be known, captain Starch gives no quarter
I've never had to bolt my door on my own ship
and I'm not going to start now bosun.
Now! be about your business man".
"Yes sir".
Smithy and Sampson knew they had to hide

until the Royal Hawk set sail
the following morn for London.

"We must stay buried in the sawdust Sampson,
until captain Starch has set sail,
listen to me and we will prevail".
Sampson started to chant,
"Buried deeply in the dust,
dust tae dust, death nae fuss,
we lie to rest in peace
and wait for death's own
secret meet".

Sampson gently placed his huge hand
around Smithy's neck and asked,
"Smithy take Sam to meet death now!
Be you go first and bring him back
tell he, I wait here in a grave, be black".

Sampson started to slowly tighten his grip
around Smithy's throat while stroking
his brow and speaking softly
as if a child were going to sleep.

"Gently rest in peace
and sleep the everlasting night
and when death comes, bring him to me
I need to know if death be right".

"Sampson ***NO! NO!*** I know where
death is, I will take you to him
when we leave this hiding place".

Sampson released his grip, and Smithy
gasped for breath.
The two lay beneath the pile of sawdust
and both had thoughts of a kind.

'Twas not long before the old bell tolled
and an old cock crowed,
and people could be heard
to work and to speak,
"Did ye hear the ghostly sound,
the sound of the bell in the night,
what - what - what, something be not right".

"Be about your business Angus
and fix my boots".

"Ah! What - what, there be ghostly goings-on
and a tale to be told
mark my words, be something eerie to behold".

All day, as normal, the work ensued,
with raging, roaring sounds and scents,
and dust was thrown on the old dust heap
where no-one knew two men inside
lay so still, yet restless underneath.

The eve bell tolled, as joyful workers
left for homes and wives and lives
the relief from a hard day's sweat,
a deep soul satisfaction,
the bones that bleed regret.

The shipyard gates closed tight
yet always open, as if to say,
'Please do not enter, yet must be must, if so,
a wondering or lonely soul may enter or may come and go'.

Soon be dark, and dark be safe
for innocent folk who need to hide
an everlasting wake.

Sampson and Smithy step forth from
their sawdust bed, to shake the dust
from clothes and head.

"Now! wait here Sampson,
I be a seeing if the Royal Hawk set sail".
Soon return, young wily Smithy.
"Good news Sam, the Hawk has gone".
Left behind, two carrion.

Soon the midnight hour,
the two men's stomachs rumble deep,
the eyes for food to scour.

"I be goin' for that cockerel Sam,
wait here and be still".

The cockerel was asleep, a continuous sleep
as the knife so quickly cut off the head
and the legs kick hard beneath, while red eyes watch,
as if to run, denial bequest
the headless chicken, watch the dance of death.

One chicken on a metal skewer,
over the dampening, hot glowing coals,
the ashes stoking heat for meat,
well! After all, they have to eat.

The chicken done well, to a turn,
the skin so crisp, the meat so white,
the mouth does drip on the carving knife.

Suddenly! Smithy's heart in his mouth,
What shocking sound? What horror from hell?
A sound like ten screaming banshees,
or, 100 fighting, howling cats,
he drops his chicken to the floor
to quickly run for the stoke room door.

What be? this sound to wake the dead,
or even, be the dead, this evil howl,
from the sawdust shed.

And there the giant Sampson stands,
with an oily, old dirty set of bagpipes,
blowing and pounding upon the bag o' air
and he, looking up unto the sky,
some secret within his own mind's eye.

"***Sampson! Sampson!*** No stop, stop,
you will be the death of us".
Smithy grabbed Sampson's arm and the two
quickly hid, back beneath the sawdust heap.

"Why Sampson? Why do you make so much noise?"
Sampson slowly mumbled, like a naughty child,
so sad and still to turn the heart
so gentle yet so wild.
"Captain Starch once told me,
when be I beat the metal pins
I be makin' enough noise t' wake the dead,
so I dinged da bell, t' bring death back".

The two lay silent for a while
as Sampson cried, with dripping tears on dust,
his bewildering, wondering thoughts no-one may know,
so simple, and yet maybe so close to truth,
as the cow's horn stabs the sandy bank
and treasure spills a twist of time perchance.

Soon be, Smithy returns for the chicken feast
and the two suck bones bare of all the meat,
then lie in wait for dawn to quake
to meet the day, and start anew
a life so instant, pick or choose,
be duck and weave, each single day to live
the hungry mouth to feed, ad-lib.

As the old bell tolled, the new day's birth,
the two lay still, and Smithy planned
a new day's start for life and work.

So still beneath the sawdust, listening like mice.
"Did ye' be a hearin' that banshee in the night?
What - what? A howlin' and a screeching',
be evil a doin' at hand, what - what?"

"Be gone with ye now Angus,
we've a work tae be a doin'!"

"Mark my words, there be something' afoot".

Soon the room was empty and the two men
arose like zombies from the dust,
with a hope the wind would blow their way
and fill their sails with luck, to sway.

Smithy turned to Sampson
and took hold of his giant, gentle hand,
"Now listen carefully Sampson,
we be a goin' t' see the foreman o' the works,
so be a keepin' silent, not a sound, shhh".

"I be as silent as the sleeping death, shhh",
whispered Sampson as he stared at Smithy's neck.

'Twas a sight for sure to behold,
as tiny Smithy walked across the yard
with giant Sampson following as told,
to find the foreman of the works,
a cockney lad so bold.

"Excuse me sir! would there be any
work for me and me friend 'ere,
I be Smithy and this be simple Sampson Simpson,
simple 'e be sir, yet do the work o' three men".

"An' what work would it be ye would be doin'?"
"I be an engineer sir, the best,
wi' steam and cogs and belts and shiny steel,
there's nothin' I can't fix, t' keep the wheel spinning,
an' this be Sampson, 'e will lift and carry
like a horse, and stoke the boiler,
or hammer in two pins as one
a mallet in each hand,
to beat and chant
be a rhythm all so grand".

"An' what dae ye be knowin' of steam laddie?"

"Well sir", says Smithy,
"the fire-tube boiler makes the steam,
for the atmospheric steam engine
developed by the blacksmith, Thomas Newcomen.
James Watt was born in Greenock
renowned for his work at the University of Glasgow.
The double-acting steam engine valve
allows high-pressure steam to act
Alternately on both faces of the piston
and ...."**Woe, woe, I kin see ye
know yer stuff laddie**"
"And I was an engineer on the 'Reindeer'
the fastest steam ship ever", Smithy had to add.

The foreman had nought to lose
and such was the way for jobs and work
the instant come or go, to hire or fire,
no workers rights or safety rules,
just men of iron to work with tools.

"Ye can run the engine, the two o' ye',
Put one foot wrong an' ye' get me boot".

"Yes sir, thank you sir".

And so it was, as Smithy skipped for joy,
And Sampson scowled and wondered what the fuss,
When soon be death to meet to sleep.
'Twas after several days, Sampson whispered,
"Can I speak?"

When Sampson spoke, Smithy feared for his life,
be a promise made to a giant's tantrum, strife.
"Smithy! now show Sampson death,
when I sleep for death to meet,
he never came, so Sampson weep
and yet death come, where ere he be,
go to sleep now, go to sleep gently".

Smithy stared up into Sampson's whispering face
as he felt his hand closing tightly around his neck.
"***NO NO Sampson***
I will take you now to see death"
Sampson released his grip, "Ooh now Smithy?"
"Yes let's go". The two left the shipyard
as the sunset sank the day
a ball of fire into the sea
soon, stars stir the Milky Way.

Smithy walked in circles around Stornoway,
no! he knew not where to find death
yet knew if he stopped walking
death would soon find him.
And all the time simple Sampson sang a chant,
"To death to meet today,
hip, hip hippy hooray.
To death to meet today
hip, hip hippy hooray".

Smithy was a savvy lad
and soon he found, through veils of mist,
a graveyard, where a shovel kissed and hissed,
the earth to dig, for some poor soul
deep into the ground, a coffin's hole.
"Stop Sampson, look!" "ooh, ooh".

Sampson's eyes stared and bulged, white in the moonlight,
"ooh, ooh, ooh".
Smithy gasped for the chance of life, reprieve.
"Look! Sampson! there be death a diggin' his hole".
And away walked Sampson to meet with death.
"Ooh, ooh, ooh".
And away walked Smithy, rubbing his neck.

"Who be there? I be Macomerat the gravedigger!"

Macomerat screamed as he was suddenly
approached by what he thought to be
a giant white-faced ghost with bulging eyes
appearing through the graveyard mist.

"Ooh - ooh, hello death, we meet,
be gravestones standing, souls to keep
if you touch me, for sure I sleep".

The old gravedigger Macomerat,
stood still, frozen with shock and horror.
Sampson climbed down into the grave
and lay outstretched, with his arms by his sides.

"Here I lay my soul to rest,
I go to sleep, now I've met death".

Macomerat was a wise old man
who had stood the test of time
and knew the laddie in the grave
be of a simple mind.

Macomerat sat by the graveside and spoke to Sampson.

Macomerat	*Sampson*
Ah! God gave thee nae wits	now God bless me
ye poor, poor laddie	poor, poor laddie I be
Why be in the grave?	Ti' hear the song of the spade
Life be quick enough to pass	ti' meet with death
death comes to all	and my mammas grave
your mother be in heaven	take me death
in a garden with flowers	to heaven to see
with butterflies so free	my mamma again, to be with me
your mamma waits	take I there, my soul
she waits for you	take I there, my soul
and only God can say	take I there, my soul
di'nae cry laddie	I want my mamma
I be with you now	I be with death to wait?
God will bless	take me ti' God
thy simple wits.	God's pearly gates
Now come with me	please take my hand
for God tae see	ti' the promised land
into the church	ti' kneel and pray
and pray with me and stay	my saviour today

Macomerat became like a father to Sampson
and every evening Sampson would pray at the church.
He simply walked into church, knelt down and prayed aloud,
he did not worry or take heed of others
if the church was full of worshipers.
Sampson would walk to the alter and kneel and pray
as he sang his distinctive chant,
"God be with me
I pray and wait
for mamma
at the pearly gate.
And bless my soul
and all who weep
God be with ya as ya go ti' sleep.

Many be the tales told of the two
as Sampson stoked the boiler
while Smithy cleaned the flue
yet no tale be told so often
as it was one tragic day, when tiny Smithy
fell into the spinning wheels
and his legs were torn away.
Two red, bloody stumps of pumping blood,
as Sampson ran from the boiler house
with Smithy held high within one mighty hand,
and Sampson shouted across the yard,
"Death be soon at hand".
Smithy's life was saved that day,
with bubbling molten tar, to staunch the blood,
with two black stumps, and days of fevered pain
Smithy arose, rekindled to remain.

So it was, with Smithy's brains and Sampson's brawn
the two did work as one,
and Smithy was to grow accustomed
to the old bagpipes, which he often played.
And at many a mighty ship's launching
Smithy could be seen, sat high upon Sampson's shoulders
playing his old ragged bagpipes.
And a tale be told of the
launching of the D.L. Mackenzie,
when all the town be there rejoicing.
Be it, when the trigger was hit with the mallet
to release the sliding cradle, the mighty ship
slid several yards before a coming to a halt.
Suddenly a giant of a man
with a whole tree trunk,
levered to the rear of the ship
and 'twas a sight to behold for the children,
a giant with a tiny gnome upon his shoulders
playing the bagpipes. And all the
while, the giant, chanting, huffing and puffing,
"Holy ram - Holy jam
Holy ram - Holy jam
Holy - Holy - ram O"
And suddenly the towering ship's timbers

creaked and groaned, as the cradle's tiny steel wheels
began to move and spin down the well soaped ways,
the giant roared and raised his arms
as the bagpipes howled on high.
The D.L. Mackenzie rumbled down the slipway
as the earth trembled and quaked beneath the peoples feet.
Then, suddenly the steel wheels of the cradle
engaged the iron rails of the repairing slip
with an ear-piercing screaming,
a mother giving birth, as the crowd cover their ears
then the colossus, titan crashes into the sea
with a deafening thunder, as the sea
reluctantly changes shape, throwing angry waves
like mountains to meet the sun and sky,
until, like a wild, tamed stallion,
the sea rumbles, grumbles and tosses the ship,
one way, then another,
to test forever, the eternal, restless acceptance,
to ride the bucking waves for joy.

The crowd roar and the children scream
"Mammy - mammy, who was that giant?
The giant with the gnome on his shoulder?"

"That was Mighty Simple Sampson Simpson
and Tiny Legless Piper Smithy".

GALLOWS HILL
Cnoc na Croich

The last man hung at hanging hill,
stole a chicken, so, 'tis said.
The highest hill in the castle grounds,
above the woods, to hide the dead,
as if death be a sin,
a sin to hide and dread.

From the bar up to the tollbooth,
with a rope around the neck,
on a placard, written, "HABIT AND REPUTE A THIEF",
so bold upon the breast.

Led through the streets of Stornoway,
Goathill, Bayhead, Point Street,
the executioner cracks his whip.
The people scorn and cry, "Be rid",
'tis a hangman's noose, for a hen,
stolen, to taste so good,
and the bitter taste left in the mouth,
the rope to choke upon the blood.

Hanging hill, the gallows high,
within the castle grounds,
be sure, during 1849,
There was very little crime.

KILDUN HOUSE

(The escape of Bonnie Prince Charlie)

Was, the Kildun House at Arnish Point,
where nought, but nought remains,
where the MacKenzies lived,
and a tale begins, 5th May 1746.

'Twas late and dark, windy and wet,
when a knock came to the door,
'who be this, at this late hour,
be the devil for to score'.

Two shadowy, bedraggled, tired and hungry men,
George MacKenzie took them in,
for food and rest, to dry the wet,
be a dram and a tale of quest.

Bonnie Prince Charlie, be scarred and bruised,
only three weeks past at Culloden Moor,
be thousands, the Jacobites last stand,
all dead, near Inverness, blood stain on the land,
William Augustus, the 'Butcher of Cumberland'.

Prince Charlie stared deep into the peat fire flames,
which danced relentlessly, no care or woe,
"What have I done?" The earth, peat, burned,
and the fire did nae, but know.

The Kildun family sat in awe,
never seen, a man, so great, so sad, forlorn,
Jacobite, tears from death's lost souls,
defeat, and yet still the taste of victory's denial,
a never ending twist of fate,
a living, dead man's, everlasting trial.

Charles Edward Stuart, Bonnie Prince Charlie,
The 'Young Pretender', knew that all was lost.
The Forty-five Rebellion, claimant to,
the British throne, young chevalier, so bold.

The 'divine right of kings', the Stuarts,
and yet this guilt within, to hide from God,
be no decree, a foreigner, born in Italy.

The seven men of Moidart,
Be the Stuarts standard raised high at Glenfinnan,
the 1745 Jacobite Uprising, rebellion.
The MacDonalds and the Camerons
supporting each the other, join the clans to rule,
by taking lowland's Edinburgh.

Victory at Prestonpans, John Cope, be gone,
the Kings army on the run, 6000 clansmen won,
and all, seemed all, so well,
beware, sweet taste of victory, chimera,
wild fox, be chase the fleeing lamb,
suddenly to face the butting ram.

Thirteen miles from London and the Crown,
reality, be stand your ground,
a persistent stare beneath deep brows frown,
this moment lived, repeat 1000 times,
What if? Transfixed in time,
truth be, turn around, back down, decline.

The peat fire burns to dry Prince Charlie's salty tears,
soaked into clay to tread, and tread through years,
the pain that haunts, and taunts,
endless cries of joy and pain,
victory, defeat, yet there be only one,
one to carry blame.

The King, once so proud, disgraced within defeat,
One moment proud, the next one meek.
Now hunted, a criminal, a fugitive,
and all, so many die, and will die, if they he meet.
£30,000 pounds. The Government Reward,
and yet, not one person told a tale,
or spoke the hidden word.

Donald MacLeod, too ask for help, escape, in Stornoway,
and many turn away with fear,
to aid a King with a trail of death,
and death still be so near.

Deep within a Stornoway inn, the hand of help,
be found,
fate declares, be always one,
to alternate predestination,
With hope and God's hand found.

Captain James

We cannae leave
the young King
from the English
to escape
to watch
be death
and yet
be brave
to save
and sail tae be
and to the boat
must hide
I know three men
to take the King
in a fishing boat

Captain David

be strong and proud
to survive
we have nae fear
be English ships
our seas
to sail
we must
our King
Ah! A small boat,
tae sea, tae be free.
some disguise
a secret be,
three men to trust
to take the King to sea
from Stornoway quay.

Callum MacAran

Baker I be
The King to sea
for Scotland did he fight
to save his life
whisper
be a fishing boat
I will hide the King
in my bread van
Ah! be tae hell
the Sassenachs

Allister na Miaran

Tailor I be
you ask too much
but nae for me
the English come
whisper
to take some bread
I admire you
Ah! Early morn
Ah! tae hell
tae war

Natty

Teacher I be
too much from me
I value life
and be the knife
whisper
Ah! I be with you
you're my friends
we shall meet
Ah! Tae greet.
defeat.

The King be no more than a wreck,
awake all night at Kildun House,
wrapped up in quilt, and staring into devil's flames,
the timeless, endless, eternal, infinite,
interminable, imperishable, everlasting,
death, yet deathless, the moment be immortal
the end forever screaming within the mind,
and nought to stop this torture,
nae, even death,
would mock one's own, debauchery.
"I cannot stand the pain, my people
die, and now I die endlessly, and nought I do,
to free the hand, with spirit to fight,
be now too late, please! Fate.
Fate be twisting as a snake,
wreathing, this way, then another, which way now?
As I forfeit, to live in burning hell,
cursed war! The endless toll of a death watch bell".

Prince	Conscience
I did what I had to do	for your people
Ay! for my people	or yourself
for Scotland	you had to win
win the battle for Scotland	and you would be King
my birth right	you were born in Italy
NO, NO, NO,	your mother was nae Scottish
NO, NO, NO,	the truth will haunt
my father and grand father	my father and grand father
were Kings	would frown upon me
NO, NO, NO,	what have you done?
I did what I had to do	thousands of Scots dead
'Twas France, let us down	blame France
I could have worn the Crown	count every Scotsman's head
we won at Prestonpans	the taste of victory so sweet
we won, we won	the moment, ever keep
please, please, oh, no,	the pain of time, time lost
Edinburgh, we conquered	victory, now the Crown
now to be King	of Britain
NO, NO, NO more	you win some battles but nae the war
NO, NO, NO more	the cries of death and loss
I beg, No more	tearing bayonets
NO, NO, NO more	deaths rotting corpses strewn
let me die	the cries of dying men
denial, the victory	denial, so safe, a hood
we could have	while every second hundreds die
we could have won	the table would not turn
we had to run	the moment of defeat
NO, NO,	to run like sheep
I should have died	to shouts of mocking scorn
in battle	yet the King, he must live on.
Sat looking into the flames	from hell
a Scottish home	nae rest, shhh who tell?
Lewis, so, remote	a fugitive, in my own land
so still	still a prisoner
flickering flames, sleep	***OH NO!*** nae sleep
you torture me	***You*** torture, ***You***
leave me be	***OH NO!*** I never go
not again, not again, please	faces, faces, faces, faces
I beg, NO, NO, NO,	remember the eyes
we fought for Scotland	the words of friends

a fight for right
the men came willing
I am within an endless death
without dying
so much death
how many tears I cry
my poor soul
NO, NO, NO,
Ah! a whiskey bottle
Ah! So sweet
Ah! So sweet
Peace, peace
Sleep, slee ....

now dead, because of you
to die without fulfilling
Yes! I cannot leave
Death - Death - Death
be in your mind
for ever
nae! self pity you murderer
YES, YES, YES,
you may hide yet, I have to return
I fade, yet never go
I fade ....
I fa ......
I ....

And so it was 'til early dawn,
when Callum's bread wagon,
led by two black horses, snorting steam,
as if this morn they know
what fate, eternal, deem.
Allister and Natty taking watch,
close by, to cover for a bungled King,
to hide away from spying eye.
Clip, clop, clippety, clop, horses hooves,
pass by, down the sleepy Stornoway streets
a fishing boat to meet.

Callum sits without a sigh,
As Allister and Natty walk ahead,
To guide a way, to the boat close by.
AH! a sudden, terrifying cry?
"What be, what, what, news, news?"
A quick reply, "Be gone Angus
or I swear this day you die!"

Down by the quay, fishing boats set sail,
Captains James and David, dressed as
Plain clothed fishermen,
"Aye, Aye, me lads, get that
bread aboard, set sail!
And speed bonnie boat, like a bird on the wing,
tae Benbecula, like a witch, with a spell, for a King.

Benbecula, so still and peaceful,
the tiny fishing boat, to dock,
at a timeless creaking, twisted pier,
the biggest catch, that ever was,
a King to be, defeated, yet still the British fear.

Bedraggled, misplaced, wandering, wondering, pondering,
misguided, deluded, beguiled, lost in death
a trophy, an emblem, an insignia,
a secret flag, alive, yet torn apart,
the King of chess, nae game
all pawns be lost, the bishops pray again,
The King remains, and stands alone,
alone in endless pain.
The last torn flag upon the hill,
held high, the battle lost,
yet every second counts,
and whilst the flag in fist remain,
one day a King may rise again,
the last man stand, as bullets tear,
into a dead man's, dying soul,
even in death, the rigor mortise,
holds the flag, courage raw,
the dead nae see the end of the war.

Wee fishing boat, as soon as dark, set sail,
the Bonnie Prince, standing alone,
on land with silent swirling mists,
as if some kind of fearful ghost,
If come upon dismiss.

A King upon his own land, oust,
Import, transfer, some petrifying, putrefying,
plague of death, to smother, stifle, suffocate
just one touch eradicate.

A King, stood alone, Medusa,
the pain, even to die, would be but to betray.
Nowhere to go, or turn, only back to France,
France who promised help, betrayed,
to grasp, at least one IF, one Judas kiss.
The King's hand, deep into his pocket,
wraps around his only cure for pain,
the smooth, glass whiskey bottle
'Thank God' a few last drops remain.

Nae, drink to remember, nae, drink to forget,
to drink to oblivion, unconscious regret,
the honeysuckle sweet perfumed droplets
dripping like the last drops of cool water
for the shadowy figure standing alone
in the burning desert sands.
The bottle smashes upon the rocks,
"Even you cannot stay, and pleasure to torture me".

Through the mists of Benbecula's shores,
faint voices whisper from over land,
"Hello, hello", a figure approach,
the prince, his sword in hand,
"Who go there?" whispers the prince,
"'Tis I Flora MacDonald, be with me
now, quickly".

Ambling through heather torn shrub,
and bush, the two flee for life,
for surely caught would be the knife.
And after endless trips and cuss,
A cottage there be, thatched and rough.

The door shut tight, the two inside,
catch breath, relax and stare,
one into the other's eyes.
To each the beauty of the other,
as if two halves, to find a match,
when one heart beats, a secret code,
some sound or scent of love from aeons past,
God's own eternal spellbound cast.

Flora's hair was long and fair,
her hands were hard and worn.
Deep wisdom in her eyes decried
conceit from a beauty no man scorn.
Her lips were full, so sweet and pursed,
as if to sulk, yet tease, to play a word,
tall, so slim, her long red dress, to fill,
did stretch, and weave, diving in from hips to waist
as crimson heather on the highland hills,
her heaving breasts, so milky white,
so pure, this priceless sight,
no price, for nature's pure delight.
And as she smiled, the prince
could feel his heart beat fast,
And this he could not understand
Afore, when his heart had beat so wild
His sword and death
Would smite a smile.
Be love and hate, and death and life
one coin spun
and only fate delight.

The young prince stood so proud,
so young and yet worn and aged,
as if he had lived one thousand years
and counted endless deep dug graves
His sword hung loosely from his side,
red blotches, stains from blood,
Flora wondered ..., turn back time,
and would he if he could.

There hands like magnets, drawn,
together, to touch, unspoken understanding,
the prince collapsed at Flora's feet,
the world turn, spun around,
for within the throngs of death and hell
one hand always be found.

Prince Charlie	*Flora MacDonald*
I cannot stand the pain	nae, Prince, you are safe,
no, I have no fear	I will protect you
I welcome death	you have to live for Scotland
I suffer with each breath	to be, a King
I live an everlasting death	to take the throne, demand
So many have died	you must live for them
if I die?	or their deaths be wasted
Victory, I see their faces, the joy	friends forever
defeat, I held men as they died	forgotten never
'Twas my fault	they died, for Scotland
I crumble and cry	and they be brave for
The pretender, what am I?	the King and crown of Scotland
A King, a fugitive	the English fear
a walking corpse	the last one standing
No, No, No,	hold my hands
the screams of death	look into my eyes
I am the cause	look into my eyes
your beauty burns my soul	now! taste my lips
so moist, soft and warm	kiss deep, I take your pain
but, but,	kiss deep and hold me tight.

The Prince did cry in Flora's arms,
someone to care, to love, to suckle,
a man as a child, emotions naked,
self-esteem and pride, torn, bare,
A King so strong an effigy,
to whom may the King bow his head?
Upon Flora's breasts, the King's tears flowed,
be secrets, only a woman knows.
The healing body's warm, embrace,
a love so pure, be rare in war,
unrequited love with no malaise.

I have never known such love
you heal my pain
please stay with me
please come with me
your beauty and kindness, love
you bring me, peace of mind
a calm, a happiness
I have never known
Be my Queen
be with me as one
together the fight to fight
to die on our feet
or live on our knees
two passionate souls
for Scotland be freed
my love so deep for you
kiss me, please
hold me, please

war has no love
but! names and graves
soon to come and soon to go
soon I shall leave
Yes! I have a love
soon to be married
I am promised to
Allan MacDonald
'tis love I feel
my doubt, be real
nowhere to go, but flee
your battle cry, oh King
yet I am at peace
to turn from war
my love, Allan MacDonald
I am confused
oh! no please no
no please no.

A peaceful love, so caring, pure,
submissive, control, fawning, servile the prince,
who need who? the stabbing sword,
to control, contort, strength, support,
adulate, revere, exalt, placer.

Tiny boat, vulnerable, delicate.
Open, towering, passive sail, down or open?
Come the gale.
Be safe, storm pass, or ride the wind,
so free.
Excitement, sensual, erotic, adventurous,
elation, lascivious. Or?
Lewd, deceitful, perfidious, recreant,
fickle. Oh no! Quisling, chased, stalked,
hounded, pursued, tracked, immured,
tortured, martyred, persecuted, tormented.
furore, tumult, anarchy, bedlam, pandemonium.

Please stay
my love
stay with me
yet, you kiss so deep
our spirits together
nae hesitate, please
My pain, you ease
and now you tease
yourself to please
I love you
I need you
please stay
I pray, please stay
my pain, my pain
Sorry, sorry,
my pain, my own,
your anger
tear my broken heart
aye! young pretender
my torture, lecture
my only company
the amber nectar

I must leave, for now
my Prince
I cannot, too much, you ask,
love and lust, to tempt,
so strong, so deep, love?
'tis not my nature.
I care, a carer
my mind, nowhere
my choice, confused,
I love you?
I love Allan MacDonald
I go this night to sleep
nae weep
'tis your pain Prince, **now stop!**
I cannot bear this plight
you ask too much
I go this night
be at peace, oh Prince,
stand tall, be strong
now I must leave
to soon return.
take this bottle,

'Tis all we may bequeath.

Flora MacDonald	*and Lady Clanranald*
My friend, hold me	what, be, my friend
my heart be torn in two	such tears you cry, what be?
Do you promise, my secret	Aye! I promise,
for the pain, too heavy to bear	a friend to share
I have been with the Prince	nae, nae, 'tis your life
I have felt his heart and pain	you risk, and
my heart be torn between	Allan, a redcoat
two lovers	soon, to wed.
What will be?	Your head will be,
If I run, with the Prince	and £30,000 reward,
to worry at every turn	who's trust, to stab,
and look behind, in fear	to watch your back
yet! to be Queen	nae! the young pretender
his spirit is good	reality, be hunted
and free	never free
excitement! adventure!	torture! death!
Which way?	Think clearly, Flora
my nature	for once, a choice be made
nae, be wild	must be until the grave.
and yet, my heart	Your heart betrothed
will nae, forget	a passing spree,
a love, forlorn	passion, nae depth,
to ever wonder, IF,	a lovers leap
IF, love be wild	Ah! So wild
what if?	with nought to last, to keep.
To keep him safe	we must be swift
from evil, death	for General Campbell
to hide and move	searches for the Prince,
to win this fight	troops be near, and leave no
to keep a new	blade of grass unturned
King safe	the hated prize, the Prince,
from England	one man, one country, England,
England, quake	with fear across the Minch.
The Prince	to France must sail
to Skye escape	disguise! a velvet veil
Betty Burke	**AH!** Betty Burke, the maid,
the big-boned maid	come! some of her clothes
make haste	to the Prince
to the Prince	for to escape.

The Prince was nought but happy,
to be dressed as Betty Burke.
"Bah! nae! a King I be,
and many names that follow,
'the great pretender'
'the Bonnie Prince'
and now 'a maid in yellow'
will my tortures fate ever cease?
And! If be I die, or caught,
in my dress, my soul, nae rest in peace".

General Campbell's Redcoats,
could be heard to shout close by
like wolves, to hunt, to follow scent
the pack, some instinct, hell bound bent.

Halt! Who goes there?
Halt! in the name of the King?
"Nay! the King I be", whispered Betty Burke.
"Have you bonnie maidens seen
The Bonnie Prince?"
"Nae, fine sir we have not".
"And what be your bonnie lasses names?"
"I be Flora MacDonald and this be
Betty Burke, and this be Lady Clanranald".
"Such beauty I have rarely seen
so pleasing to the eye,
to look upon your beauty deep
your lips so gentle, sweet.
And you fair maiden, Betty Burke
your eyes so soft and meek
why cover beauty with a veil?
Why hide a velvet cheek?"
Flora replied, "Miss Burke does greave
her father's death,
from some such plague, as may remain
to carry on the breath".

The soldier looked to Betty's feet,
"Ah! why wear boots,
upon such tender delicate feet?"
"She wears the boots to dig the field,
to carry back the peat".
"Be on your way sweet bonnie maids,
and beware the 'young pretender'
and later in the tavern be
my eyes to share your splendour".

'Twas dusk, the tiny fishing boat,
set sail, for Skye,
Three maidens and a two-man crew,
Betty Burke, with sad bowed head
swirling thoughts and feelings,
trapped within the living dead.
Revealed, beneath a petticoat
the bottle be, the spirit red.

Through the late, calm, moonlit night,
the tiny boat does kiss
The lapping waters, sea, pursed lips,
A gentle splash, a secret carried, past.
The restless, whispering sail,
a gentle breeze to tease,
a passage through the night,
where once the boat had been
the sea, so quickly swell,
to pass without a trace
an empty whiskey bottle sink
The Prince forever on the brink.

The Hebridean isles, so still, serene,
the fragile fishing boat,
docks beside a mighty brig,
bound for France, the cargo tweed,
to cover o'er a Prince's head
to still the English, wanton need.

Prince Charlie's heart be heavy,
torn, then torn with love,
"Please! Flora, come with me,
I beg of you?"
"I cannot my Prince".
"Please! Flora, this is our last chance".
"I cannot my Prince,
be it that I love you so,
my love is stronger for another,
now my heart will always wonder
'twas it one, or should one be the other".

The mighty aching, creaking brig
set sail for France,
and through a porthole, in the bow
Flora caught one fleeting glance,
a sight to haunt her very soul
forever miss the instant, chance.
Through the mist, the Prince's
pleading eyes
a tortured man, alone, loves last hope,
and even love be gone,
and even death, without a sigh
be no release
be no debate
the lonely Prince past into the night
held within the fists tight grip,
an eternal grip of fate,
and the only thing left for the Prince
be the whisky in the crate.

(Postscript) Kildun House

Was, as if a curse be left in Kildun House.
The Prince's pain engraved forever
too much, to be, soaked up within the ground and walls,
sometimes a pain so strong remain
as if so loud the sound
the echo ageless time sustain.

Secret whispers on the breeze
"Aye gone forever, Kildun House be cursed tae fate,
flat, be gone, behind the steel of the Arnish yard gate".
So easy wipe away a time
endless be, the whistling wind forever spin and whine.

Prince Charlie did leave a
blanket, quaich, and ring,
given to Lady Kildun
for a helping hand to a lonely king.

'Tis said Lady Kildun was buried
wrapped within the cocoon of the blanket
the blanket breathing from the past
bound by a steadfast, hope, through pain,
be the table turn and the past remain.

'Tis told Lady Kildun was buried
within a blanket, shroud,
soaked with the blood, sweat and tears
from a king who died, yet stood so proud.

Part Two

Tales from Lewis

'Twas the year 2000 and the ferry was due to leave Stornoway just after 8 a.m. due to a delay. The Clinton family sat waiting in their hired car - mother, father and their 10 years old son who was sat on the rear seat. The family was touring Scotland and visiting Stornoway as Cathy's ancestors came from the town. Cathy and James were tired and fell asleep in the car. Tom, their son, was bored and quietly opened the car door to stretch his legs and have a look for any boats. After about thirty minutes, Cathy and James were awoken by the haunting screech of an invading bell's toll. "Tom, Tom, where are you?" cried Cathy, panicking. Suddenly, Tom appeared at the car door. "Where have you been?" shouted Cathy, "get into the car, the queue is starting to move".

Tom quickly jumped into the rear seat of the car.

"Phew! What's that smell?" shouted Tom's father, James. Tom was dirty with coal dust and stank of kippers, gas and pipe smoke.

"Where have you been?" cried Cathy angrily.

Tom replied, "I've just had breakfast with my Great Great Great Grandfather".

Cathy and James stared, open-mouthed at Tom. "Are you telling tales?" Tom's father asked.

"No Dad", Tom slowly opened his hand to reveal a small black cross, "but I do have some to tell".

MY HERRING GIRL

An old man stood, in an old doorway,
He watched the cars flash by.
Arctic Lorries, vans and trucks,
a tear fell from his eye.

So alone, alone, in the middle of chaos.

Time changes everything, 'tis said,
my memories ever last.
I close my eyes, my thoughts to cast,
I drift into my past.
Shonag, Shonag, I miss you so!
Why did you have to go?
With yer Cota strup and Oilskins,
with yer cutag in yer hand.
As I drifted in on a drifter,
silver herring, for a Baltic land.

Almost 30 kippering yards,
blowing smoke from Kipper Road,
Kippers hanging from 'tenter hooks',
for London, to be sold.

Six days a week, most days fifteen hours.
I seen ye cry and I seen ye sigh,
I seen ye trying to stand up straight,
yer fingers bleeding, gutting fish,
I know yer back did ache.
Never a moan, always a grin.
Shonag, I miss you so.
I can see ye now! You would stand and spin,
when ye seen ma boat drift in.

The old man strolls
To South Beach Quay.
'A builder man, in a yellow hat',
"Move on old man, you're in the way".
Ah! Time changes everything, 'tis said.

On Inaclete and old Bells Road,
The kippers high did hang.
The smoke did rise to tease the breeze
to drift across the land.
And when my fishing boat came drifting in,
Shonag would grin and twirl.
She was my love, my own princess.
Shonag my herring girl.

Ah! A bench, to sit and rest.
Eyes closed tight, my memories
My memories ever last.

Silver Darlings, in a birchwood barrel,
The cooper rolls them by.
1000 herrings in a cran,
to be filled with a bleeding hand.
Stacked up high, on North Beach Quay,
waiting for the Crown's own brand.

Shonag! Is skipping towards me.
Shonag! Covered with scales, and blood and sweat,
I remember now, I can see so clear.
'Twas the eve we met.
Our lips did kiss,
The taste of salt dismiss.
'Tis now the taste of tears I cry,
I cry for the time I miss.
The rushing cars,
and buildings growing,
plastic cards for cash.
Time changes everything, 'tis said.
I close my eyes, live in the past.

The evening twilight,
cars bright lights,
Flashing, blowing fumes.
I start my walk home,
Stop! 'Tis Shonag, Shonag!
Through the shadows, a silhouette,
I rush, is it really you?
Shonag, 'tis you! You stand forever,
Cast in bronze, a cast forever last.

On Inaclete and old Bells Road,
The kippers high did hang.
The smoke did rise to tease the breeze
to drift across the land.
And when my fishing boat came drifting in,
Shonag would grin and twirl.
She was my love, my own princess.
Shonag my herring girl.

GARRY BEACH

Through a silence, of eternity?
Still, restless be the dawn
the sunset creep and peep
as if to stalk, cool breathing mist,
The breath of life,
as Garry Beach is kissed.

Golden sands of time, sublime,
Stroked by crystal water
Mother nature's healing balm,
'Tis but one place left on earth
where God does grant a quarter.

A gentle stream creeps through the sand
from peat filled hills that watch,
the stream is brown from the earth above
and feeds the Sea with love.

Tunnel, caves, walk through,
a deep carved fairy story,
the colours within the walls foretold
of time, and seas persistent fury,
like a cast from ages past
recovering in Glory.

The towering mountain face,
the gulls have made their place.
They nest and swirl above the world
as if to sing and celebrate
with endless mounds of coelenterates,
a heaven on earth, nature deliberates,
This sanctuary, as if a secret place.
I fear and pray, be beyond temptations reach
Please, God Bless, Garry Beach.

THE PEAT BOG CRAG

I walked alone one early morn,
sunrise creep,
breathe the mists of dawn.
I came upon a shadow, black,
like a ghost through the mist,
in a peat bog crag.

In a peat bog crag
at the edge of time,
a lady stood, so still.
She was dressed in black
in some kind of sack,
she was staring, at an old stone mill.

Her back was bent
beneath the creel of peat
which seemed to touch the sky.
She was grey and old,
while bright, like gold,
a flame of love, from a heart unfold.

She carried a wool-tipped distaff
which was underneath her arm,
and in her fingers
she did spin.
She was calm, as she turned to look at me
with a wry, tired, twisted grin.

I looked into her face,
the lines, so deep,
like highland hills
or mountain crags.
A tear ran from her eye
and through the valleys it did creep,
to leave her face without a trace
for to splash upon the peat.

I offered my hand, and her grip was tight,
as she stared into my eyes.
'Twas a scent so sweet, like burning peat,
incense,
whispering, endless sighs.

She led me to the edge
of a peat bog crag.
'Twas endless time below,
where happy people danced, and laughed,
and the heather, so soft, did grow.

I could feel my feet begin to tap,
to a melodeon and a fiddler's beat,
in the wink of an eye,
I was skipping high,
dancing upon the peat.

There was salted herring and potatoes,
bacon, eggs and plenty of tea.
Pancakes, scones, crowdie and cream,
and barley wine in buckets, free.

I skipped and danced at the edge of time,
I was happy, 'twas an endless spree.
The people loved, and danced and sang,
they filled the air with glee.

I danced 'til I could dance no more,
and I laughed 'til my tears ran dry.
I knew I would never be alone,
'twas the day,
when the peat came home.

When I awoke, I was lying on the peat,
the sunshine on my face.
There was a silence, no one, to be seen,
all had vanished, without a trace.
Suddenly, I could see, an old tin mug,
left full of barley wine for me.
Aaa! ha! I laughed with glee,
I would never forget the time I had,
My time at the peat bog crag.

THE WRECK AND THE RAINBOW

I walked along the shores of Point,
Newlands! New name,
Some aged place, eons could never change.

The sea, tide, anger, bashing Rocks,
like fists of salty sweat.
Every clash, thunder, sea spray high
be followed by retreat, an ache, a groan, a sigh.
As if a never ending war,
a clash of Titans,
a stalemate, rapture, for ever more.

I count remnants of shells and crabs,
a cycle of the living dead,
the rotting seagull, carbuncle,
the old ram's bleached, white head.

Suddenly, a shadow is cast over me,
I raise my head to face a tower,
a ship's death bed.
Cast out, standing on the rocks,
the blood of rust drips endlessly,
a grave, a monument to
the Glory of the dead.
Above the wreck, a rainbow arch,
a halo, crown, or the horseshoe
upside-down?
Decry, forlorn, some scrap in a nook,
frozen in time,
by the spirit of bad luck.

I clamber over jagged rocks,
seaweed and barnacles, a waste of time to cuss.
I move towards the broken wreck,
the sea, splash, grab, it's
cold and salty claw on me,
as if to catch a thief,
a thief be steeling secrets from the sea.
From a timeless shell, a memory
of some Captain's destiny.
The shadow of a death?
be incomplete, a clue be left,
one half waiting, on the dark sea bed.
'Tis a puzzle to coax a 'passer-by',
this twisted metal reaching for the sky
as if to cry, 'please lift me free'.
Spit as a bone, from the mouth
of the mighty deep blue sea.

I lay my hand upon the
rusty, cold, wet wreck.
I close my eyes and listen to the waves,
the waves that cover,
still depths dark secret.
Waves like teeth, that chop,
so trespassers, swallowed, sink,
into a limitless hunger,
I see! the fishing ship,
was tossed and thrown
in a midnight storm,
lost far from home.
The ship's crew prayed
to be saved
from the devil's lot
and a sailor's grave.
The ship did groan and ache
riding waves. My hand did shake.
I could feel the fear
and taste the salt
death's lust so near.
The Captain stood, he did not flinch,
as the ship did battle within the Minch.

Then a sailor's shout, 'there's a light ahead'.
A lighthouse beam from Tiumpan Head.
The Captain shouts, 'Rubha an Tiumpain'.
A lighthouse beam,
a dot in the dark,
a reprieve, to life, to sail,
as each man prays
to God, with a heart-stopping fright,
staring out at a dot
in a deep, dark, lonely night.

The ship's engines roar,
'tis a life or death fight,
climbing mountainous waves,
then, crashing down out of sight,
and each man does know,
for the engines to stop,
the sea's mighty power
would devour their lot.

I open my eyes to look,
I see my hand still on the wreck.
The wreck, I feel, does shake,
should I run? The ship's rust flows
over my arm red, like blood.
I close my eyes tight, I would run if I could.

I feel the rain beating into my face.
I feel the wreck vibrate.
I taste the salt.
I fear the ship maybe too late.
My eyes closed tight,
I see a light,
and 'Broad Bay' shelter
from death's own dark plight.
The Captain screams out,
'Starboard about',
as the ship heaves and crashes,
from the mountains of doubt.
The hull creaks and groans
as it twists and bends back

and water creeps in,
as its back starts to crack.

Past Rubha Bhatasgeir, Vastiker, Point,
to Rubha Meadlonach,
and a calm Loch of luck.

'Tis small, Port nan Giuran,
life and safety they dock,
yet the sea, still be angry,
to be fed, it has not.
'Drop the anchor, make for shore'.

The deserted ship still wrestles
with the sea and its plot,
fixed safe to the anchor chain,
safe and peaceful be docked.

The Boat	*The Sea*
Why?	My nature be
Why me?	You test the sea
I love the sea	my mood so free
I float above	my womb
Care free	a mother be
My hull, so hollow	Bina - to swallow
Yet, so small	her children
in a deep, deep sea	In a deep, deep sea.
You stretch, and pull and push	Come to me
So, safe now in the bay	No! No!
To sail another day,	My anger and fury, be
with you.	with you.
I lie to rest, this night,	'Tis a fight,
my plight.	my right.
What! are you doing?	Your chain,
My chain,	the anchor of life,
Be strong.	the weakest link.
Please, leave,	No!
Please, go,	No!
I feel, the snap,	Yes!
now I am lost	No! you are mine,
be sunk sublime	a monument of eternal time.

The ship was tossed and turned about,
like a twig in a river,
to a fate without doubt.
Still she fought, and remained afloat.
So, the ocean threw her on the rocks,
'twas the final wreck
of one more boat death quest.

The ship's death cry,
with tearing, ripping, screaming steel.
Torn in two,
two half's,
one below, one above,
a monument of death.
Thank God, no life was lost.

I remove my shaking hand,
from the old shipwreck,
a tower so grand.
I reach my eyes up to the sky,
where the rainbow arch's high.
The colours bright,
to reward a plight,
of a battle
one dark night.

OF LOVE AND WAR

Donald Saighdear! as a boy did ply
with line and hook, on boat and pier,
Happy lad, island dreams, no worry,
nae reason and nae need to hurry.

'Tis a mystery. How life one day, so free,
to live and play, to feel the sun,
to ride on waves, a baby bouncing on a knee.

Skip so light, the life's fandango,
Careless? island free, a dream to dream,
The new born lamb, innocent, supreme?
the wide eyes, shallow? Deep?
God's love bequeathed?
God's golden eagle, prey, a soul to keep, bereaved.

Donald dancing, know no fear
the church of God, of life and love,
Now! What be this place? This place? Crimea.

To the depths of hell,
where no man ever jest,
yet each man wonders why?
Why I be on this cursed quest?
Old 'dog tags' tied to body bags
to count a multitude of endless deaths.
When and where and here and now,
Wondering thoughts of life and death,
of love and hate,
'tis an endless queue
So patiently to wait, no need to rush,
why rush to the devil's pew?
To war, the devil's game Donald my son

Mother! To war with all my love, my son
with all my love, to kill, and kill.
With a bomb, bomb here
and a bomb, bomb there
with a bullet and a bayonet
and a dead man's stare.

The humming cold wind bites,
a bite so deep, the pain to sway,
a trench of mud so long, so long, to friends today,
how many lie beneath our feet
a dug man's grave, no soul can keep
God's consolation! Still I weep.

Only the dead have seen the end of the war.
[Plato].

Well done, your medal, hero, proud,
now carry on your life, go back,
your medal, be within a hidden shroud.

Kathleen O'Malley, bonnie round-faced Irish lass,
kind and gentle, naive, sweet sixteen,
the catholic rosary beads to count,
for countless times, the wine and bread
The crucifix upon the head.

America's soldiers, young, street-wise,
a New York lad, the gift of gab,
to swoon, Kathleen, with love and hope.
One drink, one night, one kiss, given, stolen, all.
How many times the broken heart,
broken trust, a lifetime nae repair.
A seed within, of guilt, a cuss,
the church gates closed,
To the poorhouse now, the brandished soul of love.

Magdalene sisters, to curb thy evil heart
your baby stolen for your sin
punishment upon, punishment, God's own requiem.
The war be done, if ever be,
Donald Saighdear, travelling home with friends,
to Ireland's friendly shores, visit, requisite.
A broken man, bomb blasts in his head,
hands tight, covered ears and eyes,
endless, visions of the living dead.

The whiskey, amber nectar, on an emerald isle.
To numb the pain and wash away the death.
Each new dawn, full of scorn, the cursed survivors
own immortal breath.

Donald, one day, staggering down a lonely road,
sits upon a green grass verge,
his back against a fence, the stare, to the bottom,
of the whiskey bottle.
"'Tis never ending", a voice? from where?
from the other side, of the side of pain,
which side? for the two,
one pain the same.

the fence

Donald	Kathleen
Uhh - what! my drink	Why do you drink?
to forget, to	to quench a pain?
die, escape	with the answer in
The pain of war,	the bottom of the bottle
sanctify my soul,	I am with sin
Are you a whore?	Yes, an unwed mother
Be but, a mistake	now cussed to hell
Hell be where I have bin	and where I dwell
I am so alone, behind my fence	I am so alone, behind my fence
in pain	in pain
I can forgive you	you have no sin
yet my guilt remain	you have no blame
the haunting, blood and death	the man to stab and
the bayonet, in, so deep	penetrate with shame
my soul, be in a pit	my heart to break
a never ending keep	lost trust pure hate
What be? This fence?	between the world
an evil hand	to protect from all
to hand, the gift of sin	my sin.
Hold my hand	Take now! hold tight
fair maiden, your sin	be gone from hell
no more be laden, please!	to trust! my fight!
escape with me	escape with me, tonight
hold tight my hand	a healing grasp
for life	so free
love's freedom	like a pearl white dove
all, so free from strife	can I, can I once more feel love?

Two lovers, flee, freedom pure,
escape, the smothering of dictations love and laws.
Run, run, through fields so green,
the pure water from the fresh clear stream,
new found love's eternal dream.

From Ireland, to the Isle of Lewis,
the past be transfigured and annulled.
The bond between the two, as one
inseparable, as if were one alone, be caught,
and taken back to the sanctity, the sanctity
of hell's tormenting glory.
For glory be within the war,
and the relinquishing of sin,
the brandishing, inviolate, penance
be retribution, a sanction, accorded,
and acknowledged be a ceded soul,
repent, atone, relent, with the pain and sorrow,
revealed, proclaimed, beatific, redeemed,
plied, to be, for whom, the designated
path assigned, be eternal
in glory everlasting, with endless
jurisprudence, for all, and all, always be the one.

The two did age with time as one,
yet Donald, started to the grave,
as fate predict, the tides of time,
bearing illness, creeping, malign,
or be release, a circle, interminable, infinite,
the enigma, belief and faith, blind, and yet
within the heart one feels, so deeply,
true love, a power? divine? ask meekly,
lest some mighty hand, to come,
erase, abrade, I, infinitesimal, imperceptible,
a grain of dust, an atom, mathematical?
a miniature of what? to suckle, to the bosom,
O, contain the whole within, I, the microcosm.

"I wish 'twere you, to go first Kathleen,
for the loneliness to bear, to live will be the pain".
At Donald's wake, Kathleen did cry,
"Why did ye die, why did ye die?"

No children for a second root in life,
so alone with grief, life be strife,
returned to the poorhouse where she died.
The two together now, be one
buried, side by side.
Moonlight.

A BRIDGE TO NOWHERE

There is a bridge to nowhere
Somewhere, just past Garry Beach,
A testimonial feat, of architectural craft,
Grey stone, arching shoulders,
Built forever to last.

I walked across, an honourable task,
Beautiful scenery spans below,
the peat blood river flow,
I walked somewhere, to nowhere,
nowhere, I did know.

So if you visit Garry Beach,
there be a sign just there.
'Tis to tell you how to go somewhere,
to the bridge which goes nowhere!

LEWIS CASTLE

A treeless island, bought in 1844
by James Sutherland Matheson,
to be, one of the finest woods
in the west of Scotland,
planted, growing, wild and free,
towering glass houses, filled with
exotic plants from nations far across the sea.

30 acres of forest, for an island
where never be, nae trees.
A pseudo-Tudor Lews Castle
some say one of life's folly's.
£40,000 to cost, to build
with stone from Dolley Quarry.

Lady Matheson and Mr Matheson, a baronet in 1851,
For the Lewis people, saved,
1845-46 he fed the people
saving all from an early grave.

Lord Leverhulme, the castle bought in 1917,
'Twas sold in 1924, with a gift left to restore,
the parish of Stornoway
including all the woods
the castle grounds, nae out of bounds
left for the peoples trust.

1939-45. WAR.
With the devil, time and fate nae wait,
death be at the door.
For the lives be lost
in a timeless cost
war's everlasting score.

The castle, a naval hospital,
times of war, do change us all.
The towering glass houses, are no more.
The castle grounds
grow wild,
'tis nature free, a jubilee
nature's born free child.

Birds fly free, in the castle grounds,
in the harbour and foreshore.
Flowering plants, shrubs, ferns and trees
leave be, for evermore.

The legless, lizard, slow worm,
like a snake, harmless
does roam and squirm,
and may bask in the sun on rocks,
as if to live without a care,
as if no outside world be there,
such freedom, be so rare,
Away from all the world, and war,
a riddle I think, for who could ask for more.

I look around the castle grounds.

Blackbird, Blackcap, Brambling, Bullfinch,
Bunting, Buzzard, Chiffchaff, Chaffinch,
Corncrake, Crossbill, Crow and Coot,
Dipper, Dove, Cuckoo, Curlew,
Golden Eagle, Fieldfare, Flycatcher,
Dunnock, Gold crest, Goldfinch, Oystercatcher,
Heron, Hobby, Owl, Moorhen,
Martin, Merlin, Mallard, Pigeon,
Kestrel, Kingfisher, Jackdaw,
Pheasant, Sis kin, Peregrine,
Skylark, Snipe and Sparrow.
Sparrow hawk, Starling, Stonechat, Swallow,
Mistle, Thrush, Tits - Long tail, Coal, Great and Blue,
Redpoll, Redwing, Plover,
Yellowhammer, Tree creeper, Wagtail and Twite,
Warbler, Waxwing, Woodcock, Whitethroat,

Woodpecker, Wren, Wheatear, Whinchat,
Cormorant, Dunlin, Guillemot, Fulmar,
Diver, Gannet, Kittihawk, Merganser, and a
Partridge in a Yew tree.

Patience, please, and now some trees.

Cedar, Cypress, Deodar, Hemlock, Fir,
Hiba, Larch, Pine, Juniper,
Silver birch, Box-elder, Alder, Ash,
Aspen, Beech, Chestnut and Elm,
Ash-leaved, Wild cherry, Holly,
Hornbeam, Laburnum, Hazel, Lime, Laurel,
White beam, Walnut, Spruce, and Yew,
Rowan, Sycamore, Maple, Oak.

Yes! Just to name a few.

Lewis Castle

(The Original)

The ferries gently come and go,
where once the castle stood,
people bustle to and fro
where once the battles toll was blood.

I often think that in the sea
the arrowheads still lie
and I often hear the ghostly sounds
of the Vikings battle cry.

1100 standing so tall and proud, Lewis Castle,
the battlements rising high above the land,
built by the MacNicol family
from the Vikings to make a stand.

The Norsemen came for 'Steering Bay'
the best natural harbour Stornoway.
Led by Leod
the battles raged the cost in blood, Odin,
Valhalla reign, the castle turrets
beaten, molten tar, and battering rams,
giant boulders catapulted,
arrows, swords and shields revolted.

The MacLeods of Lewis
settlers be, a clan of Vikings from the sea.
Through the 1500s restless warriors,
with a nature to fight, to die with sword,
confront the power of Edinburgh, dissension
1597 James VI proclaimed the hidden word.
The Fife Adventurers sent to destroy the MacLeods
to maraud the barbarous Gaelic-speaking word.

After many battles 1608.
The MacLeods defence victorious.
So few against so many, the Vikings ruled the sea.
The long ships, Odin's, red and white stripes,
behold with fear the axe, the sword, the knife.
The Vikings ruled the mighty waves
and James the VI, grieve, bewail, lament,
deplore, rue, mourn the countless graves.

1608 James VI withdrew forlorn, disheartened,
Overwhelmed, thwarted, vanquished, dismissed,
Distressed, dismayed, appalled, mellowed,
Be all, with all, so few to stand so bold.
The bull's horns helmet 'STAND FAST'
The sea be red while the Vikings laugh.
1653
Alas time moves to turn the mighty wheel,
Stornoway Castle, destroyed by Cromwell's
mighty endless armies.
1800 times last remnants removed,
erased, dejection, despondency,
decease, demise, lost forever, missing,
mislaid, strayed, misplaced,
wayward, vanished, such disgrace,
violated, disregarded, infringed, transgressed,
for a terminal pier
be the ferries to rest.

The ferries gently come and go,
where once the castle stood,
people bustle to and fro
where once the battles toll was blood.

I often think that in the sea
the arrowheads still lie
and I often hear the ghostly sounds
of the Vikings battle cry.

THE BLACKHOUSE

Move from the caves, souterrains,
Crannogs, duns and brochs,
to build from stones, turf and driftwood,
God bless the floating log.

Seaforth's officers claim
the shores driftwood
with a letter 'S' marked in red,
'tis a poor man's blood.

The Comptroller's tour of inspection
for to find stolen driftwood
and if even charred black
on a chimney stack
would be taken
for the sake of good.

Gather round neighbours, lend a hand,
a house built in one day,
by evening time, drink barley wine.
Now! a fire, 'tis twelve months we will stay.

Tighean geala, white house,
built of stone and lime
to stay and sway the southwest wind
to stand, the test of time.

Forty, fifty feet in length,
by ten or twelve in depth,
with a fosgalan porch
and a toll-fhasgaidh, hole
for grain to be winnowed.

Rounded walls of undressed stone,
with a slant
to ease the rain,
six feet in height
with a thick ridge pole
to support a thatch of turf,
or sometimes
rushes, fern, heather and straw,
or potato shaws were used.
No Nails!
Straw or heather ropes
to bind a steadfast home
to earth.

Hugging low, the ground
the wind, to blow, like a mouth
'Curse you, O south-west wind,
you always search out a ropeless house'.

'Fuadach ort a' ghaoth an iar-dheas,
'S tu gheibh lorg air tigh gun shioman'.

The byre, inside, to share,
Dug a few feet deep, for cattle and sheep,
a mire to fill, the hoofed feet beat,
creelfuls of smùr to still
Dry turf for the dripping wet, to seep.

A fire
in the middle, teine,
two inches high,
packed with stones, in a cartwheel rim,
through the farleus, roof hole high
peeping at the stars and sky,
to rise, some of the smoke, so grim.

"The black peat will warm itself
before it warms anybody else".

Above the fire hung the slabhruidh
from an old ridge pole
two couples high
swung an old pot-hook
for a pot to cook,
the children would swing
while the flames danced high,
't would burn their toes
an' make 'em cry.

Turn the peat, to make some light,
the home made tallow
for a candle bright.
Strips of cloth in an old clam shell
fish oil wicks
the dark night quell.

Sitting on a pile of peat
or a large stone by the fire,
a cold winter evening closing in,
the cow safe in the byre.
Food served for all, on a wooden clàr,
the ceiling, sealed, with peat-bog tar.
The family circle
God's golden ring of life
the flames, entwine, uplifting love
carried on a spiralling, smoking, twist,
through a peephole in the roof
to the shining moon above.

"Is abair á nís gach tigh, teine mor is deagh bheann".

"The cause of joy in every house is a big fire and a capable wife".

LORD OF THE ASHES

Ashes to Ashes

1735, 'twas the beginning,
to slowly bleed the land
the seaweed rich
'tis manure the land demand
Soil so poor, while the seaweed rich
your bleeding blood
from the fields
like ashes, nothing yields
Sea-wrack
so slowly burnt
the peoples land
our lives, to live
you bleed us dry
for, money, cash
and all be left is stashes
on baron fields

Hugh MacDonald
of Baleshare
rich from seaweed
and an endless amount be there
AH! £30 a barrel
dripping, dripping, residue
the kelp, the iodine
'tis free I will nae share
Sea-wrack
my residue
the ashes left
my need, to need,
my residue, the barrels feed
until all wrack be gone
and all be left is stashes
of empty barrels

all be left be
Ashes to Ashes.

THE RAIDERS OF PARK FOREST

Sir James and Lady Matheson,
turn away this day, 'tis discontent,
the peoples desperation, poverty, starvation,
a pit, a trap, a corner, without ultimatum.
God bless the Queen,
nae, for the rich to see, or know,
the earraidean, estate messengers,
the carrions of death,
the leach, Donald Munro,
autocrat, despotic tyranny,
'tis Donald Munro,
"I'll deprive you of your land"
my factors, ground officers, the earraidean,
only answerable to her Majesty the Queen.

The carrion fly low this day,
for 56 Bernera, crofters families,
the year 1874, summons from Munro,
56 Bernera families, homes and land to go,

The cultivated land, for food, the need,
now taken for sheep, 'tis wool and meat,
the wheel of change
what change for the poor and meek.

O to rise you landless men of Loch's,
your children starve
while the wealthy gorge, the honeysuckle sweet,
to climb and crawl
to choke the land
a cancer beat the barley wheat
and by the way, your venison tastes so sweet today.

Schoolmaster of Balallan, Donald Macrae,
the landless men of Lochs, to lead,
the invasion of Park Forest,
where the deer do graze
on poor peoples land, for the rich,
the venison, so grand,
and by the way, your venison tastes so sweet today.

The 22nd day of November 1887
this be the day,
the landless men of Lochs, to rise,
from Crossbost and Gravir
100 men step forth for Seaforth head, to meet
a passion bourne from an empty gut,
the need, for children food to eat.
God fearing people, kind, gentle, meek
now take to arms,
muzzle-loading rifles, spars, sails, cooking pots,
stones and sticks and rocks and bricks.

The Raiders of Park Forest
you landless men of Lochs,
this day, to be, your day
led by Donald Macrae,
for the poor man's fight
be the rich man's plight
and by the way, your venison tastes so sweet today.

Park Forest soon was taken,
poor people danced and sang,
boiled and roasted venison
dry bones spit on the land.
The taste of victory so sweet.
Sweet venison, the food of life,
the hunger, crave, the rich man's meat.
behold the carving knife.

Now, sat at one-eyed Donald's Shielings
with guts, so full to burst.
Sheriff Fraser reads the Riot Act
and the crowd slowly disperse.

Dear Raiders
the 13th of January 1888 the prisoners
Deer Raiders,
for the high court, on the ship, S.S. Lochiel,
bound for Edinburgh
bound fast to an even keel.
Deer Raiders
found not guilty,of mobbing and rioting,
heroes carried down High Street, high,
by jubilant, rejoicing crowds,
returned back home to Stornoway,
deer raiders, heroes, men, so proud.

Starving families and children, led by
Donald Macrae,
and by the way, Munro, a man who has no heart,
your roast venison tastes so sweet today
to the Raiders at Forest Park.

THE RIOTS OF AIGNISH, POINT

At the old eye churchyard, Christmas day, 'tis 1887,
The people meet, fighting talk, 'tis leaven.
Primed by the Raiders of Forest Park
and a need for fertile land.
Mr Newall, you Raven, by the people told,
He had two weeks to move
to move his cattle, from the fields at Point,
or every beast would be driven away
to be roasted on the joint.

Mr Newall, took no heed,
be not his children's mouths to feed,
to fight, Newall's fences and dykes destroyed,
his stock allowed to stray.
First blood, baton of the law, one man caught,
one man, locked away
imprisoned at Stornoway.

A crowd gathered at Aignish farmhouse,
Mr Newall produced a gun,
the crowd dispersed, and disappeared.
Ah! the battle was far from won.

The date was set to raid the farm,
9th January 1888.

500 men and women, hunger a desperate need,
around a flag, at the top of
old Knock Hill,
this day the law, take heed.

The Royal Scots moved in,
to quell the angry crowd
and H.M.S. Seahorse eased into
Sandwick bay, marines to fight.
The blood to spill upon the fields,
sweat and blood, the food of life,
life be an endless strife.
Lawmen waiting at Aignish farm

led by procurator fiscal Ross
the raiders stormed
at the break of dawn
to chase, from the farm, the stock.

Sheriff Fraser appealed to the crowd, to stop.
About High Noon, the battle fought,
each Scot to fight a Scot,
with sticks and stones and rifle butts
yet all, but all, was lost.

11 prisoners locked in a cell,
the incensed crowd, did try to free,
The battle raged throughout the streets,
once peaceful, the streets of Stornoway.
"Fix bayonets" was the cry,
"for law be law, even if you all shall die".
Point folk fighting on a bayonet, point,
"No surrender", was the cry,
the Riot Act be read, out loud
to a peaceful peoples, angry crowd.

The Royal Scots moved in
and the crowd was soon dispersed,
for stones and sticks cannot be quick,
against a rifle, and the bullets click.

On the morn of the 13th January, 1888
H.M.S. Jackal did set sail,
with the Aignish men who fought for food,
to Edinburgh to face Lord Craighill,
a judge in a dour mood.

12 to 15 months in gaol,
but nae to break a Point man's soul,
the heroes of the landless men,
who fought to live,
who fought, to feed their kin.

LEWIS

To live upon the golden isle,
to watch the sunset creep,
to see four seasons in one day,
where the sun and moon both meet.

The clouds float by, on a canvas sky,
above a moonlit, shimmering sea.
Wild rivers flow, rust red from peat,
with pools, so clear, so deep.

So many lochs, and each one, calm and silent be,
to mulch the peace throughout the land,
true colours and true harmony.

People, calm and friendly, ask nought,
yet offer a helping hand.
On a Stornoway street, the people meet,
Nae, 'tis not a barren land.

The wheels of change come rolling in,
and usually, pass on by.
'Tis a one-way street where the past repeat
with the eagles, free to fly.

Lewis and *Change*

Lewis	*Change*
I am at peace, leave be	from the world
I be no part of	the wheel of change
what spins and weaves	will turn and turn
'tis greed	to feed an endless need.
You dig my skin	to build into the sky
and drink my blood	to fish the waters dry.
Temptation be	you take my food
Temptation be	you take my cars
Temptation be	you take my fuels
The island a jewel	I am no fool
to treasure	my need must feed
for the world to keep	an everlasting need
I grow so old and tired	I grow and I need your space
to fight 'tis not my way	with battleships and jets

'tis peace, fulfil
'tis peace and love
the last hope faraway
A cancer, you spread
a leach, you suck my blood
Only once the change
my life be gone forever
The sheep, the peace, the heather

I will take and kill
I have, I do, I will,
your island be mine to stay
the more I have the more I need
but, the need is good
for now, I grant a quarter
now live, I take a measure
my revenue a treasure.

Turbines growing in a field
spin the winds, for a power refine,
please keep the island
'tis one last place,
a bubble trapped in time and space.

HIGHLANDS

So still. The rolling, flowing highland hills.
The eyes free glance, a drama to behold.
'Tis Scotland's skin, heather clad,
Gliding downwards, what tale unfolds?
A woolly old time beard,
or a chain of flowers from a blooming lass.

Great walls of power rise, to block the sun
shades, the changing browns and greens,
'tis God's own canvas,
'tis the spinning wheel of dreams.

Wild, burly heather spitting colours,
crimson, purple, yellow,
sensuous scent, sweet musk,
the scattered jewels of Scotland
sprinkled like stardust.

Down in the valleys, water twists with glee.
Waterfalls and bubbling streams.
Some trickle, while some roar with rage,
a task, to fill the sea.

The morning mists, from the stretching,
sweating earth.
The morning dew, each globule,
a pearl, a diamond,
clear crystal through the sunlight twirl.
Mother nature's sweet caress,
'tis the beauty of
the Queen of Scotland's dress.

The majestic stag, stands so proud,
antlers, branching, to stroke the sky.
Pumping, snorting, steaming breath,
a twinkling depth, within a staring eye.

The eagle, soaring,
rides the wind,
unchallenged, even man can only look with awe.
And like an arrow, darts at prey,
an angel of death,
with hanging talons, to warn all beasts,
of nature's cruel, eternal quest.

The cool, calm trout patrols,
endless depths of lochs and streams,
hunting flies and bugs,
fulfilling patient fishermen's dreams.
Rainbow colours, wild sea, and brown,
the fly may dance upon the loch
But he should nae look down.
Plop. Plop. Upon clear glass surface water's top.
Plop. Plop. Another fly is lost.
Plop. Plop. The circles suddenly spread,
as if to escape, the poor fly's fate,
the skipping fly now dead.
Must be! Something? Some secret?
The salmon only knows.
A sacrifice, a lifetimes plight.
To climb and twist and jump, so high.
A panic, for to spawn away
life's last gasp
at the end of a long lost day.

The sunset sinks into the Highland hills.
'Tis where all seasons may visit, in one day.
A place which rules itself,
where all invaders come and go.
Where rainbows float, so free,
so many, I have never seen!
Is this the place where they be made?
God's own eternal dream.

ISLAND BOY

Island boy, Island dreams
far across the sea.
Wealth and fortune, happiness,
to live a life so free.

The rocks beneath my feet,
to stand for all eternity,
so safe, this ground, my home.

How can I look, to see the sea
then turn away, yet still feel free.

My heart beats deep
within my chest.
The hot sun burns my face,
the sea spray kiss so fresh and cool,
I lick my lips! Reality.
Am I the everlasting fool.

Perchance to sail the deep Green Waves,
the Mother's cradle sway,
or, Neptune's anger, furious be,
too many spirits, hidden graves,
within an endless sea.

To live my mundane life. So free?
Upon this barren ground.
I stamp my feet.
I cut the peat.
I watch the sheep.
I do the barley beat,
and then, I pray my soul to keep.

I turn my anger to the sea,
where a temptress beckons unto me,
to challenge life, the Gods and death
for an eternity.

I stalk the docks of Stornoway
a deep lust driving, craving,
no more to walk the land and hills,
a sea man, all pervading.

Ahoy there boy! Step aboard,
for tomorrow we set sail,
you are now a Myrmidon
for we hunt the mighty whale.

Aye captain! This be the life for me
but I thought, the laws that govern us,
state that the whale be free?
The captain of the ship am I
and what I say will be,
to ride the waves and taunt the sky
we chase the beast that's free.
Then we set our coarse for Iceland, cold
where wealth for us will be.

That eve 12 sailors, and I be one,
we drink the drink and smoke the smokes
and tell seafaring jokes.
They tell of fortunes far away,
of wealth and happiness,
of women's ways I never knew
that filled me so, with lust.

The following morn "Set Sail"
at last, now a sailor I will be.

The light blue sky, the rising sun
peeping through sea breathing mist.
Such wondrous beauty have I missed.
The sea so calm, the breeze to stroke
the towering sail.

As gently out they float,
stood on the fields, his Mother waves,
while father tends the sheep.
The son so proud, an adventurous man,
but his Mother she does weep.

We had been sailing many hours,
when from the crow's nest came a shout,
"Whale ahoy, man the Guns",
and the ship turned
hard about.

The mighty whale, so free
sailing, just like me,
deep heavy sadness in my heart,
is this worth my wealth and lust.
Suddenly a mighty 'bang' an arrow shot
as the whale pays for my lot.

So close to the beast.
I feel I could reach and touch.
The whale's eye stares into my soul,
as it blows with deep disgust.

More Guns blast, the spears to cast,
a hunt for life is become.
Wild men scream, and pull on ropes,
'tis death's chameleon.

Suddenly, the whale does dive,
and I swear he winked at me,
he saw the tears run down my face
and drip into the sea.

Machinery screams as if in pain
And giant cogs do break,
steel lines snap
and the ship does heave
in the beast's almighty wake.

I see a man's arm snap in two,

And the captain yells, "Cut free".
A steel line snaps
like a taught whiplash
and two men die without a cry
Forever lost at sea.
Within one beat of time.
Stillness and silence.
A calm before the storm,
and each man reconciles his destiny,
brave men mumble prayers,
and a man screams, "God save me".

The captain yells, "The beast does rise",
And we all stand, froze in fear,
each man now silent, deep in prayer,
within the rage of death's despair.
Dante's hell. Rising from the hidden
depths.
The men gasp for breath,
as if their last.
A seagull cries, as if impatient to feed
on dead men's hearts and dreams
the carrion of the sea,
the beak that tears, no mercy shown,
in this, the place sailors call 'home'.

Bursting from the silent depths
like an atomic bomb's almighty crest
rising from the Ocean bed
as a tower of dignity.
At its peak the whale did stop
for an eternity.
A vast shadow, cast upon our boat,
and a man cried, "Pity me".

Like a mountain falling from the sky,
the whale's revenge began,
as ten men stood with open mouths
Transfixed in Armageddon.
The next thing I remember,
I was flying through the air,

like a bomb blast, crash,
or a thunderous clash,
and a boat, no longer there.

I hit the sea with a mighty splash,
I must have sank, six fathoms or more,
I believed my life time, be in vain
with every inch of my body in pain.

My eyes close tight.
I await my fate.
To pay for my mistake.
'Tis now too late to turn the clock
on youth's tempestuous haste.
As if standing in the water,
I close my eyes and hold my breath,
with my lungs about to burst.
I await my final sigh of death
yet for me there will be no hearse.

As if within a deep, dark hell.
YES! I feel a rod, a bar?
I grasp my lifeline,
whatever this -
a dead man's hope
the dead man's luck to kiss.
I grasp onto the bar,
hold tight against my chest.
The sea begins to sway and heave
into a mighty waves white crest.

As if within a second
I am rising from the sea,
rising high into the sky,
and I believe death's justice,
now a wake, to face a chancery.

I am so high, up in the sky
as I grasp my rod from God.
Suddenly, I stare into an eye,
'tis the whale and death we rob.

I grasp the spear shaft,
and ride the whale
like a mighty beast from hell
we explode back down, into the sea
with a screaming, siren, yell.

I feel as if a God on high
as I ride the almighty beast,
he groans and moans
and blows and snorts
and mocks the death
We both defeat.

I look around the waves,
yet no life there remains,
a sunken ship with a crew's death list
and eleven more sailors graves.

An eon past
the whale be at peace, we rest.
Like a desert island castaway
my fingers frozen, locked, on a rod of steel
I gasp deep breaths
I stare around
can all of this be real?

The whale has four rods stuck into its back,
from the spears of humanity,
yet fate can wait
and procrastinate,
'tis nature's harmony.

I pull the spear with all my might
while the whale did groan and puff,
like a giant pin in, a cushion of love,
my hands lock tight
I will not deter
I will recur
'tis God's will
my Excalibur.
I had to take my knife,
from deep within my belt,
I cut the whale free, from the rod,
Yes! I felt the pain he left.

Soon all the spears, cut free,
and once again the whale
did wink an eye at me
as if with a kind and gentle motion
like a giant submarine, submerge,
he slowly sank, into the vast,
Atlantic Ocean.

Alone, floating on the waves,
of a timeless time,
bobbing like a child,
within the mercy of God,
nature's womb? or tomb?
I see some wooden debris floating by.
Such a simple remnant
from a shipwreck, Ghost,
the remaining host
one lost soul's barbican.

Soon, the darkness cap, the day,
the daylight gone,
to end this way
delirious I talk, my last parley.

I feel my floating, last hope,
slipping from my grasp.
Within this cold darkness
gently sinking into an abyss
as a pebble in the sea, be cast.

Sea breath spray, my last lament,
so cool, while burning in my chest,
life's visions swirl,
spiralling, within everlasting
hidden depths
trapped within a womb? or tomb?
Mother, son's caress.

I force my last breath
from my lungs,
while watching bubbles
rising free, rushing to
escape my fate,
my last life's ebb I see.

The waters fill my chest
I try in vain, my final breath.
Sinking deep beneath the sea
to face death's final quest.

I feel so numb, and all is dark,
as I sink within the sea.
I see one thousand million faces,
and each one comforts me.

So suddenly a burning light
within the deep, dark depths,
an angel's face comes close
to me, a kiss from God's
own breath, a kiss of life, I feel
my lungs and
suck a breath of air.

A burning pain within my chest,
as I take one gasping breath,
Just one breath, to escape from
Death.

I am in hell, God dam my sins?
The blinding red, burning lights,
from the furnace fires
of purgatory's endless fight.
A devil's breath, a gale of ice,
a storming wind,
I am pulled, yet pushed,
my body will be quartered
as I pay for my past lust.
I feel hands pounding on my breast
as Satan's demons, do their best,
to tear my heart out from my chest.

I can take no more,
I scream aloud
choking in vomit and blood.
My eyes open wide, I will fight,
I will not live in hell, as I should.

A man screams words, "He's back".
And as I look above his head
a whirling blade spins high.
The sea's below, a swinging line,
I am rescued
just in time.

The helicopter man, looking at me said
Loudly above the whine,
"Been having some fun, have you son?"
I replied,
"Yes! A whale of a time".

THE RISING OF THE RAZOR FISH
(a children's tale)

'Twas George Morison told me the tale,
of the rumbling of the Razor Fish,
as we sipped our tea
over a biscuit dish.

When the sun was high
and the tide be low
a distinctive sound
would grow and grow.

From old Broad Bay
within the sands so grand
the Razor Fish became
a crackling band.

The long thin purse-like shells
would rise from sandy depths,
to meet the day, with a crackling cleft.

Be thousands, as an army, on the shore
a distant, Zulu booming march,
and many be for the cooking pot,
a tasty feast, a fishy crop,
the children laugh, snap, crackle and pop.

So! if in the silence of early dawn
you hear a 'boom', please! feel no strife
for it simply be no more,
than the Razor Fish come back to life.

STORNOWAY SHIPYARD

The shipyard's cracked old bell
to sound, another day of toil,
some say heaven, some say Hell,
so sad, the shipyard gone forever now
left, only tales, to tell,
to stroke an old man's brow.

The sweet perfume of belching steam,
to mix with coals black soot and smoke
from the stokers dreams
like clouds do float.
Horse drawn wagons, piled high with canvas sails,
from Sandwick's Canvas town,
so pearly white and brown
the smell from the canvas mountain,
suddenly laid out, spread flat
as a field of waving, weaving,
restless grass, so placid and inept
until, suddenly! filled with mighty nature's power,
so vulnerable to tear,
so passive, the wind to impregnate,
and yet the power, invisible to the stare.
The ship, with the power of a Majestic Queen,
beauty, direction, transference,
a power to move ten thousand tons
and yet, be one, tearful tear, succumbs.

The smell of the rope
as thick as the arm that tugs,
from Seaforth, ropers road
to coil and twist and weave and wind
through creosote, the nostrils sting to breath,
curled like a serpent, waiting
for an anchor's deep, dark grave
or to breach the mighty towering
masts and sails
be riggers aloft to test the staves.

At sea, the old crows nest, on the high mast tip,
where a young boy stands alone
to sway from side to side,
as if to shake or test
this heaving beast, which creaks, and aches,
a living, moving, test of human craft and skill.
The ship does toss and roll,
an itchy fly upon the nose
the lookout grips to keep his pose,
on top of the world
in the old crows nest
king for the day
the beanstalk, sail the milky way.

At Stornoway shipyard
skeleton frames of wood stretch up to the sky
surrounded by towering, makeshift scaffold,
alike the gallows high.
The musical sound of raindrops
on an old tin roof
carpenters tapping hammers, mallets,
caulking iron, adze and maul,
the chisel, saw and axe, steadfast and moored
to keels, beams and decks, land lovers
be bilge-blocked and securely shored
hammering cast iron pins and studs to all holes bored
the carpenter's cradle,
raised and drawn by many a hand
to the 'chant of time'

"RIO! RIO! RIO! RIO!

Heave ho" Heave ho!

We're off to the Rio Grand!"

The engine house alive,
a mighty dragon belching steam
spitting fire and brimstone.
Cradle, mighty spinning wheels
metal cogs, to spit and flick,
oil and grease, and WAIT! in anger
to trap a careless hand or can of oil
as if the beast be trapped
within an endless turmoil of toil.

The oscillating beam, a tornado, with winds that twirl,
the governor with its spinning balls,
lazy and limp then suddenly alive!
spinning wild and fast
awoken by the steams
raging, almighty blast
brains and brawn
a sudden ear-piercing scream
echoing some wild cast engineering dream.

To balance, tame the mighty beast,
raging power and fury, stand in awe perceive,
from silence, still, calm, stationary,
thoughts, perceptions, logic, ideas.
Four vertical spinning metal balls,
to rise or fall, perfect control,
pulsating, vibrant, oscillating,
a whip to tame the raging bull
from thoughts and plans,
progress? regret, regress?
the old hand crafts
as pyramids now, no one know how,
a twisted stern be a broken bow.

There be a tiny square of light
as if, some prison, cell window,
shadowed by a giant axel drum
to pull a mighty giant's chain
to haul a ship, from an early grave,
upon two rails greased with soap, whale fat,
to ease the trip, to the hot tar vat.
The steam driven capstan
holds its giant chain, red with rust,
peeping through the tiny hole
a giant predator, waiting for a time to heave
when lever pulled
the steam begins to breath,
a deep belching **Hoof - Hoof - Hoof**,
with strength to move
the invincible Sphinx.
And the strongest men
tartan titan warriors
the men beat the chain with mighty mauls
its locking links, to free
to beat and chant for the deep steam bass
Hoof - Hoof - Hoof - Hoof
Chink - Chink - Chink - Chinkety - Chink
"Come on lads loose the chain
wi' sweat an' spit, chant lads chant".

Hoof - Hoof - *Chinkety chink*

"Raise the sail to catch the wind
tae travel the sea sae free
and there be a lassie in every port
AY! AY! land lovers we be".

And at the back of the engine house
The black sludge pond used to feed
the 'slip boiler' from a rusty old cistern,
shadowed by the towering chimney.
Boys would revel, caper, frolic, romp,
imagine and invent, reverie in fantasy.
An old tin bath to sail the seas,
with sticks for swords,
to fight the mighty dragons
belching steam and risking life
from nostrils, pipes,
AY! good old pipe dreams.
Diving high from the hoisting beams
into mountains of sawdust shavings
a gallant knight, to save a queen.
Ah! Why be? time change everything.

The sawmill! Wide, broad, belts
to spinning, fly wheels
softly buzzing, as the tightly wrapped
velvet touch, strokes,
an endless kissing, hissing
purr of satisfaction.
SUDDENLY! ear-piercing, screaming,
as spinning, wild toothed saws
meet rolling logs in the sawpit trench
the top sawyer stood
so proud aloft the moving log
the aromatic, charming smell of fresh cut wood
the sap to drip sweet, sticky blood.

The gigantic, hulking, imposing, ponderous,
grindstone, shaping, wood,
from the softest yielding touch,
a craft and skill be ever lost
figureheads to bows aloft.

Seams to caulk and pay,
from the giant cauldron, full to brim
the pitch-pot-black bubbling broth,
a witches secret magic brew
the stench of molten tar
no water nae pass through.

The steam-stove to supple
saps the wood
to curve the planks to shape
for bows and hulls
a flowing beauty, she, the ship,
the taunting sway
the stern curved swaying hip.

The many smells and tastes
of timber, tar and rancid grease
of sweat and steam, of soot and rust and dust.

Alas, the shipyard be no more
the old rails lifted during 1934
yet sometimes .... as I pass the spot
or walk around tarmacadam's covering, new ground,
I close my eyes .... I swear I can smell
the old shipyard
and hear the sound of the old cracked bell.

IOLAIRE

Stornoway's most tragic moment, 1st January 1919,
when all folk celebrate, families to reunite
back from the war, 205 Lewis men in sight
cheering, sailing home on the Iolaire,
homeward bound, to the safety of the harbour,
loving families cheering loud
to sheath the bayonet
be all the killing done,
the ship to dock, true love to lock,
to thank the Lord for 'lady luck'.

The ship Iolaire suddenly be wrecked
and 205 men drown and meet with death,
while families watch, hearts stop, astound
within a silent shrouded shroud
no sound.

Who knows or says or questions
the hand of fate predestination, providence,
destiny, stolen, purloined, to test assess
some demon demonstrate, some evil power,
authenticate, substantiate,
when all is all, we stand upon the shore
helpless, exposed, abandoned, forlorn,
defenceless, vulnerable. Defence, denial,
victim or perpetrator, punishment, guilt, revenge,
wondering, conjecturing, inquiring,
why?

LOST AT SEA

White horses ride the raging waves
Go brave into the night.
Wild dolphins jump and sing with glee,
the sailors angels, flying free,
for there will never ever be
but one lost soul
no soul, be lost at sea.

The sea salt made from tears,
the moon, tide, change, repeat,
a never ending clock, yet restless be,
the moods, the moods upon the sea,
sometimes, so calm, at peace, to stroke, to kiss the brow.
Sometimes, a raging fury, to strike and smash a bowing bow.

Tempestuous, like life, so vulnerable, the unexpected,
for the hand of fate, we wait,
sometimes there be, but, No debate,
as the world turn, around, and around.
We dance, the dance of life,
skip, to miss the pavement cracks,
perchance, 'tis life, to live and one time die.
'Tis ours, some say, to nae ask why?

True love, and faith and God,
sometimes, so hard to see with eyes,
yet what be in your heart will last.
Yes! last for an eternity.
For true love never dies.

White horses ride the raging waves
Go brave into the night.
Wild dolphins jump and sing with glee,
the sailors angels, flying free,
for there will never ever be
but one lost soul
no soul, be lost at sea.

FAREWELL MY FRIEND

Farewell for now, take care my friend,
Ah! I know this busy life spin around, nae end,
some peace, Wordcatcher, catching words for you,
rest, to be, ah! take a time, to read a few,
from dreams, Wordcatcher,
I wish your troubles quell
For you, a book, as a coin in the wishing well.

The Wordcatcher dreams tonight.

Colin Demett

Wordcatcher

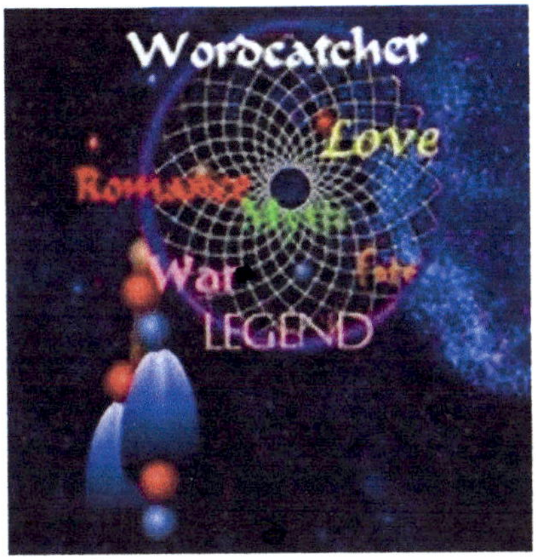

Wordcatcher Publications

Books and Verses

Unique verses for all occasions.

www.wordcatcherpublications.com

Books and Cards handmade and printed
on the Isle of Lewis, Outer Hebrides